The Medical Billing Home Business Bible

Paul G. Hackett
"The Medical Billing & Transcription Mastermind"

New York
MMX

ISBN#: 1451588488

EAN-13#: 9781451588484

TABLE OF CONTENTS

Preface

Being active in several forums, chat rooms, organizations, and answering many phone calls it is apparent that people are interested in starting a medical billing company but have several questions that weren't being fully answered therefore leaving the questioner with even more questions.

Today more than ever it seems that those that have the knowledge that the beginners are seeking in these forums are not answering them, giving half answers, and referring them to posts answered several months ago leaving them to go through several pages of information.

What many people don't understand is that these forums are run by very busy billing center (BC) owners that aren't able to sit and write out step-by-step instructions and answer their questions in full (in time you will come to appreciate the roles these gracious people serve, so don't knock 'em). The purpose of this book is to fully answer the most asked questions that you have posed in a forum, chat room, message board, and to me with regard to starting your own medical billing business.

Until recently I was the owner of Stelo Medical Management Incorporated located in Queens county New York. When I started in this business I had absolutely no clue of how to run a business, what medical billing was, or that physicians actually used billing to get paid for the services they render.

In 1997 my girlfriend enrolled in a career institute to learn medical office management and as things would have it, the school closed down. She found a new school and while helping her study for an exam I was exposed to the process of insurance, billing and accounts receivables within a medical practice.

I have always been money driven and open to moneymaking opportunities and I saw this as a way for us to go into business but had no idea where to start!

Needless to say, I had more questions than a little-bit. So, I started my quest for knowledge and it took more than a year and a half of thorough research and planning before I felt confident enough to set my plan into action. I also took classes in billing (part-time) and my girlfriend went to a specialized medical billing/coding school, took the CPC practice exam, and passed the national certification exam in coding given by the American Academy of Professional Coders (AAPC). Together along with a close friend we formed a business structure and became incorporated in October of 2000.

One morning while debating with a doctor about the usefulness of billing firms on an AOL message board, I was told that I had some insightful ideas and that I should consider writing a book aimed at helping physicians understand that they need to run their practices more like a business and increase their bottom lines. I began to think if I were to write a book I would do better helping those interested in this field just like the people that helped me.

I am not a gifted writer so you will see that I answer questions just as I would if you were my friend in search of advice. So there's no technical jargon or unnecessary fluff like exactly how many HMO's, PPO's, and Insurance companies there are in the U.S.. I will say however that you should become familiar them, as time goes on in the business.

Chapter 1

Is There A Market For Medical Billing Services?

There are several reasons that create openings in this market and as long as you can gain a physicians trust, communicate with the office staff, attend billing seminars, keep yourself abreast of the trends, and vigorously advertise the benefits of your firm you will find there is more than enough physicians in this market for you to make a good living. **I am not however saying that it's easy as pie convincing these physicians to grant you the opportunity to pitch why using your service would benefit them.** This part of the business can literally break even the most upbeat personality and lead you to quit before the magic happens.

Open any phone book and look up Physicians (in New York it is the second largest category next to restaurants). I know what you're thinking! Just because there are thousands of doctors in any given state it doesn't mean there is a market for billing services. Am I right? Now turn to the medical billing section (you might be referred to billing services) and see how many billing companies are actively advertising. In one of the prominent NY City phone books there is only 27 billing services compared to several pages of physicians.

Let's use some common sense. We know that not every practitioner needs to outsource their billing because they have an in house billing staff or they do the billing themselves, But Wait!

This sounds like an opportunity to me and I hope it does to you too. Anyway, if there are 2000 practitioners in a geographical area and you guesstimate that 50% of them do their own billing, and there is 27 billing services that means the remaining doctors split equally each service would bill for 37 doctors. Now lets be real, out of the 27 billing services there are probably about 5-8 of them that are controlling the majority of the remaining 50% of physicians. As hard to believe as it is the remaining services are probably content with the amount of physicians that they bill for or are not aggressively trying to win over new clients. So the 5-8 companies could be doing just a marginal job at billing, while signing even more doctors, charging higher prices (even to their present client base) and living well because there really isn't any competition for them due to the lack of creditability of smaller firms. Ohhh, it gets better folks.

Even in this age of technology there are practitioners that still bill for their services on paper (HCFA 1500's). Some of my most difficult prospective clients are to old fashioned (or should I say to cheap) and stubborn to upgrade their practices and use the excuse that they feel that things will go wrong if they release control of their practice to an outside service. Their own office personnel are looking for other jobs (hospitals, medical billing companies, unions, etc.) behind their backs because the amount of work can be very frustrating and the pay doesn't warrant their energy.

I personally know several medical billers and their average pay is between $18,000-$27,000 a year depending on the size of the practice and the amount of days worked per week. I also have friends that work as billers for my competition and they are getting between $20,000-$30,000 and that depends on their experience and seniority. Other friends of mine work for either city or private hospitals and they are paid $27,000-$39,000 depending on the average for the position, experience, and seniority.

The bottom line is if a physician/practice is not paying their billers what they are worth for the job that they do the quality of work and the attention of the biller begins to breakdown thus, impacting the practices revenue stream (as if there aren't enough normal hindrances that hold up payments).

Once the biller finds a new position things at their former employer is left in shambles because for ages now physicians have distanced themselves far away from the running of their businesses to focus solely on patient care. That's Right! This is yet, another opportunity.

To make matters worse for physicians/practices is the fact that they have been losing money year after year due to drops in insurance payments and higher malpractice insurance. It's a fact that in 1997-1998 some practitioner's were making $300,000 per year and today that number has fallen to about $170,000.

On January 1, 2002 physicians faced yet another 5.4% drop in Medicare payments. What does this mean to us as billing services? Well, I could say it would be harder to sign doctors because they are not gong to want to spend for my services.

However, instead I will tell you that now more than ever you need to be in front of prospective clients alerting them to the fact that you could actually be saving them money or helping them to streamline their operations compared to the way he/she is accustomed to doing business.

For example the doctor is presently spending the following to process his/her claims:

$18,000 per year for the medical billing staff

$30,000 per year for the office manager/billing supervisor

$200 per year for envelopes

$1200 per year for stamps

$1200 per year for phone calls

$500 per year for consumables (office supplies)

$ 51,100.00 per year total

(those are not the only expenses to take into consideration but this is just off the top of my head)

Now, if they were to outsource their usual 100 claims a week to you instead for processing and you are charging $3.00 per claim:

$14,400 per year for your services

$30,000 per year for the office manager

$50 per year for envelopes

$400 per year for stamps

$600 per year for phone calls

$250 per year for consumables (office supplies)

$ 45,700.00 per year total

THAT'S AN IMMEDIATE SAVINGS OF $5,400 PER YEAR FOR THE PRACTICE. So, Yes! Yes, there is a definite market for your services as long as you are willing to continuously explain and re-explain the benefits of your services to the no time having, stubborn, sometimes plain arrogant, and know-it-all physician.

Chapter 2

What Kind Of Knowledge and Training Do I Need?

Let's see… I could say it depends on the type of billing services (submission only/claims only, claims and follow-up, or full practice management) you are conducting for a client and I would be correct in doing so.

Today, physicians are coming under extreme fire from healthcare's regulatory commissions for mistakes that they and their billing staff made during the billing process. These practitioners are paying back thousands of dollars to insurance carriers because of these mistakes and some are even barred from submitting future claims through them, which permanently damages the practices revenue stream.

In an attempt to protect themselves and their investments practitioner's are looking for credentialed office or outside personnel to insure that they are in compliance with the regulations set by the healthcare committees.

With this in mind I feel that regardless of what type of service you are offering it is best to get educated (and I'm not saying some 2-4 year degree), get certified by a reputable accrediting organization, do some field work if possible, attend several workshops during the year and join a few billing organizations to keep yourself abreast of the ever changing insurance rules and regulations.

This will lend to your creditability when you begin to market your services especially when you are in competition for signing an account.

Not to mention **the more educated you are about the industry the more confident and comfortable you will be in front of a physician** when explaining your services (plus every now and then, you will get an account to sign for more because they believe you to be the most knowledgeable about the industry).

Billing courses and schools can be found in the phone book, newspapers, online, local colleges, or next time you're in a doctors office ask the medical assistants (MA's) where they got their education and more than likely the school will have medical billing classes.

<u>Please, be aware of the companies that you find online as well as those correspondence courses that are advertised on TV and those medical billing opportunities you read in the help want section of the newspapers!</u>

Understand me, I know you want to get started ASAP to accumulate all the dead presidents you can but MEDICAL BILLING IS NOT A GET RICH QUICK-MINIMAL WORK PROFESSION!

This is the turning point for most people thinking about this industry. If you begin by short-changing yourself on your knowledge, the insurance process, compliance issues, and inner workings of a physician's day-to-day operation, <u>YOU WILL FAIL</u> even if you luck up and get off the ground!

You can take a course online run by a woman who was instrumental in helping my staff and me by giving us personal advice when we were at our wits end in the beginning. You will find that I don't endorse people or services in this book but **I am endorsing the following online medical billing training course because it's the best I've seen yet.**

Mrs. Tammy Harland is her name and she runs the Medical Billing Course, which supplies those interested in billing with all the necessary training, software and certification resources.

The course is inexpensive, they will teach you everything you need to know about **medical billing business ownership,** how to be a **qualified medical biller,** and you take the course at your own pace until you complete it.

97% of my students take this course and most go on to be success stories in the home based medical billing industry. Visit my website for a complete breakdown of why I like this course compared to the other 30+ online courses I have personally taken and reviewed:

medicalbillingbooks.tripod.com/medical-billing-training-courses.html

There are two other aspects we should take a look at before we move on, your knowledge of computers and software. You don't need to be a wiz at computers to be successful but you should have a good understanding of the basic functions and hardware that came with your computer.

If you still have your manual skim through it, read up on those things you're not familiar with, and practice using them until you are. I also suggest that you read up on how to keep your computer running at optimal performance (running error checks, scan disk, disk defragmenter, scheduled tasks, disk cleanup, and data compression agents).

The next thing is software (billing software, contact management, desktop publishing, auto-save, etc.). You should be an expert at the billing software you choose and the only way to do that is to practice using every function.

Most software vendors sell a basic and advance learning video that will take you through the inner workings of the package you buy. My suggestion is that once you have used the trial versions of several software vendors and have chosen which one fits your needs best you should order the basic video first.

This will give you the chance to really understand the full capabilities of the software since you will be able to follow along using you computer as the video is playing. Another benefit to doing this is that you will be able to use your newly found knowledge to compare the other software packages (who knows you might find that another package would work better for you instead).

There are several software packages other than billing software that you can purchase that will help you maintain your business such as:

1. Contact Management-software that helps you keep track of clients, schedules, sales, histories, and other functions that you might need to know about a customer. Examples are: ACT, Goldmine, Maximizer, Microsoft Outlook, Microsoft Access, and Lotus Notes.

2. Desktop Publishing-software that helps you create professional looking sales fliers, brochures, newsletters, and pitch books. Examples are: Adobe Publisher, Scribus, Serf's Page Plus, etc.

3. Accounting-accounts receivables software helps you create professional looking patient/practice invoices and statements, print checks, apply accounts payable and accounts receivable credits to specific bills, tax forms and reduce bookkeeping errors for your company (your billing software package should be equipped to handle the accounts receivables for your physicians). Examples are: QuickBooks, One-Write, and Peachtree.

4. Auto Save-software that automatically backs-up your work from the possibility of file loss or damage, file corruption,

hard drive crashes, and virus attacks. This replaces the need to purchase a tape drive and tapes for your computer to save the work you processed during the day.

In no way am I saying that all of these elements should be in place before you get started. I am saying that you should keep abreast of what's out there and purchase them so you can make your job less complicated and more efficient for your company and it's clients.

Chapter 3

What Should I Look For In a Billing Course?

This can differ from school to school or course to course and the amount of time spent on each part will also. I do however firmly agree that even a basic course should cover the following:

ICD 9-CM

CPT-4, HCPCS, and E/M Coding

Medical Office Procedures

Physicians Billing

Documentation/ Healthcare Data

Billing & Reimbursement

Electronic Medical Billing

With competition and lack of employment growing in the NY area many folks are turning toward starting businesses they can do from home. The friends that I told you about before that have been in the field for 4 or more years without a formal education in the field are going back to Saturday school or night school for 4 hours from six months to a year to become certified through one of the two accredited organizations called the American Academy of Professional Coders.

Once the course is completed they are scheduled to take one of the two national certification exams that takes about 5 hours to complete and once the candidate passes they are awarded the title of Certified Professional Coders (CPC) or Certified Professional Coder-Hospital (CPC-H).

The other organization the American Health Information Management Association works almost the same way but has 4 different certification programs called the Registered Health Information Technology Program (RHIT-a 2 year college degree program), the Registered Health Information Administration Program (RHIA-a 4 year college degree program), the Certified Coding Specialist (CCS), and the Certified Coding Specialist-Physician-Based (CCS-P). When scheduled a candidate may take both CCS certification exams but not on the same day.

If you have experience in coding inpatient records or coding the hospital portion of ambulatory surgery and emergency room care, you should consider obtaining the CCS certification and if you have performed coding in a doctor's office, clinic, or similar setting, you should consider obtaining the CCS-P certification to backup your abilities.

Everyone else I know in this industry is either a CPC, CCS/CCS-H, RHIT or RHIA and is using their credentials as a marketing strategy with great success against other billing companies that employ what we call "robot billers" (those individuals that were placed in front of a billing program and told put this code here and that code there, then press this button, but has no clue as to what has happened, why it's happening or why it's being done).

The aforementioned information is for those that want to become employed in the workforce as a biller/coder. I just thought that I'd mention it because a lot of people ask me what they would need to do and where they can go to get further information about the coding aspect of the healthcare industry.

While there are no Federal, State or City regulations that state a person must be certified to perform the function of being a medical biller I just wanted you to know the tricks that some of my friends use in their home based businesses that allow them to differentiate themselves from other medical billing businesses.

Please remember that they were already in the field a while so they just took their education to another level and then used it to their advantage when they started their home based business.

You don't need to go through all of that to own and run a home based medical billing business. All you need to do is get properly educated about the business and the processes of medical billing and you will be off to the races.

I do suggest though that later on you look into expanding your education in the coding arena because if you do then you'd also be expanding upon the types of services that you could provide potential clients (which means more money!).

Chapter 4

**If I'm Only Processing Claims Electronically Why Do I Need
To Know Medical Terminology, Coding, Etc?**

That's a valid question! Now let me ask you one. How many
successful businesses do you know of that only offer one service?
As a business owner you have to build and broaden your services
in order to keep up with the evolving needs of your clients
(sometimes even identifying and creating the need for your
additional service is necessary to create new forms of income
from one source).

Today you might only be submitting claims electronically for a
few physicians but what will you do if one decides that they want
you to take on the coding of charts, conducting periodic internal
audits to insure compliance, or just taking on the roll of full
practice management? Without being educated how will you go
about holding on to your physician that is screaming for your
help and you are powerless to do anything.

What will you do if you are granted a pow-wow (a sit-down) with
a prospective client after you have told him how you can help his
practice and you're a Certified Medical Billing Profess-ional and
they ask you a situational question to test your communication
level, knowledge of terminology, documentation, and
billing/insurance procedures like:

"I saw a patient recently complaining about xxxx and I documented it as XX in their file, and did a LLL to relieve the pain. I then chose 12345 as the CPT code and 123.4 as my diagnosis on the patient encounter, submitted the claim and the claim was denied. Where did I go wrong?" Don't laugh, because this happened to my Chief Operations Officer not to long ago while trying to land a major hospital gig here in NY.

So, when I tell you to learn everything you can about billing, the industry, your competition, and how you will continue to expand your services take it to heart and learn from our mistakes.

Remember this! You will never be able to answer every question to the satisfaction of your prospective client but you should be responsive (listen-Don't Talk), be quick on your feet, answer confidently (even if you're not 100% sure), and admit if you have no clue instead of making something up to save face.

With that being said, I want to clarify that I am not saying that you must learn everything at once. You should however take a good basic course to build a firm foundation on and add to it by continuously expanding your knowledge and vision for your business' sake.

Chapter 5

Sometimes I See The Terms Medical Biller and Coder Mentioned. What Is The Difference and Will It Affect My Income?

The difference is rather simple and yes, it will impact your income depending on the type of service you provide a physician. I am going to begin with coder/coding because it is a specialized part of the billing process.

The last time you went to a physician he listened to your problem and proceeded to write in your chart. What he is writing is a formula called "S-O-A-P" which stands for Subjective-Objective-Assessment-Plan. He is actually converting what you say and plugging it into this formula along with his observations, conclusions, and treatment of your problem.

When that chart is given to a coder it is their job to read the chart, match up the problem with it's corresponding numerical code from the most current ICD-9 book and assign the proper diagnosis code with it's numerical code from the CPT 4 book. Those two codes and any modifier codes that may need to be used to better describe your problem and its treatment are placed on a patient encounter form or superbill. The patients chart is then re-filed and the encounter form/superbill is given to a medical biller.

Don't allow the above description to lead you to believe that this is how it is done in every practice because the majority of physicians will do the coding themselves directly on an encounter form/superbill.

Once the encounter form/superbill is given to a medical biller it is their job to input that information into whatever form of software package that is used by the practice exactly as it is written.

The next step is to either print a HCFA-1500, UB-04, or ADA form to be sent by mail to the insurance carrier or electronically submit the claim to your clearinghouse or directly to the insurance carrier.

A medical billers responsibility does not stop there because they also have to follow-up on each and every claim to make sure that is paid. Sometime that can be a burden because they have to spend a lot of time on the phone with insurance carriers trying to get information about specific claims that come back rejected or denied.

The other problem is that they also have to deal with patients throughout the day that have concerns about their bills (and let me tell you something, they're not calling because they're happy). The next area of responsibility is the accounts receivable process where the insurance company sends back the physicians payment and explanation of benefits (EOB's) for posting.

The biller then becomes a bookkeeper to keep the practice's finances in order while creating patient invoices for any monies that is owed to the practice for any co-pays, co-insurances, and non-covered services.

If a claim is denied it is also the billers responsibility to appeal the claim by getting any necessary paperwork needed to get the claim paid and resubmit them to the proper agency.

As if that is not enough a medical biller that runs their own service has to contend with the physicians that are always calling because they have discrepancies with bills, reports, or just to gripe about how he/she feels that they should have brought in more money during that billing cycle.

Oh yeah, before I forget a good biller must also make sure that the patient encounter forms/superbills that are being used are equipped with the correct CPT 4 codes (and ICD-9 codes if they are listed) to avoid any coding errors on behalf of the physician.

This is another reason that you must be continuously involved in workshops or involved in medical groups so that as changes are made throughout the year you can quickly advise the physician and correct any forms that may apply to their specialty.

As you can see a medical billers life can be hectic enough with only one physician that sees a fair amount of patients per month but imagine what it would be like if you bill for six different specialties. The funny thing is, to a biller who loves this business even more than the money the amount of work is never an inconvenience.

Now, to address the impact either/or will have on your income. If you are only going to be a medical billing service you will not be doing (or should not be doing) any coding so your income will be what you normally charge for your services. If you become certified as a coder and a physician wants you to code and bill you will far exceed the norm of most billing services because you will be charging for two separate functions (this is why I say get the education and certification so you can branch out once you establish yourself as a billing service).

If you become certified and decide to switch to only coding for physicians you can charge $25 an hour and up. I have a friend in PA who is a freelance coder that has three clients (two internists and a group practice) and he charges his clients $75 per hour, works out of his home and 4 hours a day any three days out of a week he chooses in the group practice. When my girlfriend worked for one of the largest hospitals here in NY they employed a freelance coding consultant from out of state for $90 per hour for 8 hours a day 4 days a week until completion to revise the superbills and go through charts looking for coding errors in certain departments. Needless to say the hospital had to pay back a sum of $2.5 million dollars in misappropriated funds back to Medicare because of over-coding and several other mistakes. As a medical biller or coder you are only held to the limitation of your imagination when it comes to your income.

Chapter 6

What Kind Of Services Should I Offer?

There are three packages I feel that most new billing services should offer that allows them to give great customer service to their clients.

1. Submission of Claims Only –This is when you input the information from the patient encounter form/superbill into your billing software and submit it (electronically or paper) to either a clearinghouse, the insurance carrier, or print a copy to be mailed to the insurance company.

Anything done beyond this point will be handled by the doctors office. This is rare but you will bump into a few physicians that will ask you to do it (business wise to a practitioner it doesn't make sense to pay a full time billing staff and then employ you to perform this singular procedure creating another expense for the practice).

2. Submission of Claims With Follow-up –This is the same as the submission of claims only with the exception that you will be responsible for the tracking of each claim until reimbursement is received.

*Note-with the first two packages you have the opportunity to charge for additional services that the physician might need done from time-to-time such as:

Evaluating and correcting the CPT 4/ICD 9 Codes used on patient encounter forms/superbills, the resubmitting of rejected claims, conducting appeals on denied claims, printing and mailing patient invoices, printing and mailing collection letters, printing and mailing birthday, holiday, or thank you for your patronage cards.

3. Full Practice Management –in this package you (the billing service) are in charge of the entire practice from the evaluation of CPT 4/ICD 9 Codes used on the patient encounter forms or superbills, verifying patient eligibility and benefits, making sure applicable managed care authorizations and referrals are on file for the services, gathering and entering of patient demographics into your practice management software, submitting of claims (electronic and paper), follow-up, reports, checking of EOB's, posting payments, providing secondary and tertiary claim sub-mission when applicable, collections, resubmissions, appeals, patient calls, and mailing of any patient statements and invoices.

Each practice has different needs so you should also be flexible with the services you offer. From time-to-time I research my competition to see what extra benefits they are offering to see if there is something I have neglected to incorporate into my business. You will not be able to (or even want to) do everything another company is doing but make that choice with your client's future in mind.

Chapter 7

How Much Do I Charge and How Much Will I Make With My Billing Service?

As you can tell, these are two separate questions but I feel that they go hand-in-hand. After researching for more than two years I have seen these questions answered in many ways and most of them are very misleading. I say that you should price your services according to type of practice you will be billing for, the type of service you will be giving, and the amount of time you will have to spend rendering the service.

In other words, you will have to be flexible with your pricing structure without selling yourself short.

I Know! I Know! That doesn't help you right? Well, I didn't understand it either when I first got started but it became abundantly clear once I started to sit down with clients that having only one price will lead to no income at all. So, I had to do some research on what my local competition was charging, what the NY average for medical billing services were and then figure out what my high, mid, and low price would be.

Look at it this way. If you were trying to sign an elderly psychologist who wants you to submit and follow-up on the claims only, sees a total of 30 people a month with the majority dealing with Aetna insurance, and it would take you about 20 minutes total per month to get their claims paid would you charge themas much as a practice that you have to do triple the work in order to get reimbursed? I think not (but there are those who do)!

When I say check what your local competition is charging I mean go to their website and see if they list their pricing (if not at least take down their address, major selling points, and services), ask your doctor what he/she is paying to have their claims processed, ask the office manager what company they use and a ballpark figure, go to different billing forums and post a question asking what your city/states average per claim fee or percentage being charged is, ask other local billers what they charge.

You will be surprised that the majority of services charge about the same thing in a geographic area (in NY I find the going rate is about $2.50-$4.00 per claim, 6-10 percent of the amount collected per month, or a flat fee rate of $1,500-$2,500 per month).

Another thing is, competition does play a part when it comes down to pricing especially when you are new and not as versed in front of a client (my associates may say differently but I'm just a few doctors away from being new to this industry so I clearly remember what it's like).

First off, you're excited and nervous about getting in front of a practitioner, you are not a well established company, you don't have a particular talk track down yet so there is a lot of stumbling and uneasiness, and you're not confident enough that your knowledge and pricing is competitive enough to clinch the deal.

But not to worry, with practice and time the situations and questions will become second nature and you will begin to surprise yourself. **I Can Guarantee That.**

There are going to be times that you will go below what you normally charge for your services because of direct competition (it's either you or them and you both are offering exactly the same thing). My advice is to do it only if it is not going to cost you more to process the claims than you are getting paid to process the claims. For Example:

You are charging the practitioner $2.50 to process the claim but if it actually costs you $2.70 to process the claim then regardless of the circumstances it's not worth it.

So, since each practice is charged differently there is literally no way for me (or anyone for that matter) to calculate what you will make. **Beware of anyone or any opportunity that gives you a definitive dollar amount as to what you will make!** People in this industry will ballpark for you what they made during their beginnings and probably last years earnings to give you a sense of growth potential.

I have friends that during their first year they were fortunate enough to sign several practitioners and by the end of the year they earned about $75,000. I know others that bill only for specific specialties (internists, urologists, surgeons, etc.) that earned $150,000 during last year. I know a competitor of mine that not only bills but also sells their own software and they earned about $680,000 last year.

I was not as fortunate as others and it took me almost ten months worth of learning how to market my company properly to get my first client. In early 2000 I ballooned to over six practitioners (mostly because of the flyer's I sent out when I first began and follow-up calls) and I earned just shy of $100,000 without sign-ing anyone new. Since then we have been blessed to outdo our 6% a year business plan growth goal and with the addition of the sales generated from this book we earn almost half of what our competitor makes that does billing and sells software.

As I said before as a medical biller or coder you are only held to the limitation of your imagination when it comes to your income.

You can bill, you can code, you can audit, you can become a consultant, you can teach a class, you can write a book, you can go on the touring (speaking) circuit, you can invent new billing software, you can open several locations around the nation, the possibilities are endless. Always be looking for opportunities to broaden your business' vision and you will find it to be truly rewarding and fruitful.

Lastly, anytime you feel that you are at a stand still don't give up.

Think about all the successful people you admire and all the obstacles that they had to overcome to be the icons in business they are today. You will find that the spark that made you want to start your own business in the first place will burn brighter and give you the fuel you need to continue your quest.

If you need someone that will understand your situation turn to any of the medical billing forums that I have mentioned and you will find the answers you need. **JUST DON'T GIVE UP BEFORE THE MAGIC HAPPENS.**

Chapter 8

Do You Have An Example Of A Pricing List?

To make things crystal clear here is an example of how a company may configure their pricing schedule (you can add or take away any item you wish and price it accordingly):

Submission of Claims Only

$3.00 per Claim

Reviewing of Claims

Transmission of Claims (Paper and/or Electronic)

Generation of Transmittal/Rejection Reports

Other Individualized Services Are Listed On The Following Pages

Submission of Claims with Follow-Up

$4.00 per Claim

Reviewing of Claims

Transmission of Claims (Paper and/or Electronic)

Generation of Transmittal/Rejection Reports

Follow-up Each Claim Until Payment is Received

Other Individualized Services Are Listed On The Following Pages

Full Practice Management Service
all overages are an additional $0.50 per claim

0-3000 claims:	$6.50 per claim
3001-5000 claims:	$5.50 per claim
5001 + claims:	$5.00 per claim

or

6.5%

of Monthly Collected Revenues

Reviewing of Claims/Entering of Claims

Transmission of Claims (Paper and Electronic)

Generation of Transmittal/Rejection Reports

Checking of E.O.B.'s

Posting of Electronic Remittance Advice

Generation of Accounts Receivable Statements

Weekly and/or Monthly Activity Summaries

Generation of Aging Reports (30-60-90 Days)

Generation of Patient Collection Letters

Birthday, Holiday and/or Thank You Cards

All Appeals and Resubmission's of Claims are Conducted at an Additional Charge-See Other Individualized Services on the following page

Other Individualized Services:

All Appeals Conducted on Denied Claims
$3.50 per Appeal

Resubmission of Rejected Claims
$2.50 per Resubmission

Aging Reports Generated (30-60-90 Days)
$2.00 per Report

Each Patient Collection Letter
$1.00 per Letter

Each Birthday, Holiday and/or Thank You Card
(Includes Postage)
$2.50 per Card

Chapter 9

What Kind Of Software Should I Buy?

Besides "How do I get started?" this has got to be the most fre-
quently asked question. The answer however isn't a cut-and-dry
one because it really depends on whom you plan to be billing for
(doctors only, dentists only, or chiropractors only, etc.), and what
is best for you and your business but here are a few guidelines to
follow:

1. **Only** take software suggestions from those that are truly
knowledgeable and experienced in using several types of
software.

2. Asking several questions will allow you to consider and
research several products in order to make an educated decision.

3. The type of software you purchase will depend on the service
or services that you will offer. If you plan to just submit claims
only, for your entire career as a biller then it makes absolutely no
sense to purchase a package for full practice management.

4. Your software should have the ability to expand or be
upgraded (with little effort and without great expense) in the
event you start out doing claims only and want to move on to full
practice management.

5. You should be comfortable with the software. It should not be
a hassle or over-complicated for you to figure out where to go,
which screen you left off at, which screen has the info you need,
or where you should store all the info in order to submit it.

For example: My Chief Operating Officer demoed almost 15 different software packages and compared the ease of use to the systems that are used by hospitals (like IDX, Eagle, Medical Manager).

You see hospitals are upgrading to almost human error proof platforms with screens that follow a logical pattern of events so that it makes it hard for the operator to leave out information or input information that doesn't make sense compared to information that was already input. After that then a decision was made.

6. **YOU MUST BE ABLE TO GET TIMELY TECH SUPPORT.** The vendor of your choice should offer you some sort of technical support for a limited time to assist you with setting up your software and to answer any questions you may have without you paying a fee.

After that you should be able to purchase a support package that will cover you on a per call basis, quarterly basis, six month term or yearly contract. During the demo phase you should test the customer service and reaction time of the vendor so you aren't left out in the cold when a real problem arises after you purchase their software.

Not only should you call them but you should email, fax questions to them and record their response times. Use these recordings when deciding which software vendor you are going to deal with.

Your software should allow you to:

a) Handle multiple practices/practitioners (whether claims only billing or practice management).

b) Submit electronic claims; print them to file (for batch transmission), or print claims directly onto the appropriate claim form using your printer.

c) Handle multiple fee schedules (such as Medicare, HMO Plan A, PPO, Aetna, etc.).

d) Conduct easy search queries (this brings up certain data that you have already typed and stored so you can easily point and click instead of retyping or when you are looking for data you can find it without having to exit the screen you are already working on).

e) Conduct accounts receivable functions (for practice management). This will allow you to keep track of several things such as: posting payment, adjusting balances, bill the patient for their amount, track unpaid claims or charges, and generate different reports for the practice, etc..

f) To contract with any clearinghouse you want to. This way you can shop around for a clearinghouse that fits both your needs and budget.

Chapter 10

Where Do I Start Looking For Software Vendors?

Here are a few software vendors that you can research, demo their software, and contact with your questions concerning what the computer requirements are in order to run the software effectively.

Software & Website	Phone Number
Lytec www.lytec.com	(800) 735-1991
Medisoft www.medisoft.com	(800) 333-4747
PMX3 www.synergymis.com	(800) 652-3500
AS/PC www.dbconsultants.com	(610) 847-5065
HP Plus Pro www.healthpac.net	(800) 831-9419

Software & Website	Phone Number
AltaPoint www.altapoint.com	(888) 258-2552
Kareo **(Web Based)** www.kareo.com	(888) 775-2736
Visionary www.visionarymed.com	(888) 895-2466
DAQ Billing www.antekhealthware.com	(800) 359-0911 (Ext.# 5)

As I said in the beginning I am not endorsing any of theses software vendors. I am just telling you which ones are known to be reputable in supporting this industry.

Chapter 11

Should I Buy Into A Medical Billing Opportunity?

I am by trade a salesman and very cautious about business opportunities. That's not to say that every opportunity is a scam but you have to be extra careful especially when your feelings and dreams are involved because they tend to cloud your judgment.

Knowing that fact, there are companies out there that prey on those trying to better themselves and their economic situations. These companies use your desperation, savvy sales pitches (made to accentuate shortcomings and bolster hope for a difference), convincing testimonials (usually lies), and low pricing to snare their victims.

So, before you find yourself taken in like the hundreds of thousands out there:

1. Visit the **Medical Billing Scam Watch Forum** at medicalbillingscamwatch.yuku.com. View all the posts/topics (especially under the title **"Is It Hype or Is It Legit?"**).

2. Visit the Federal Trade Commission (FTC) and see if there are any negative reports filed on the company in question. The federal trade commission states that you should be aware of several warning signs, including the following: high pressure sales tactics where the offering company does not want you to take the time to investigate the offer completely, representations of extraordinary profits with very little risk or training involved, excessively high or very inexpensive start-up fees, and lack of

communication or evasive answers concerning the service or product.

3. Visit the Better Business Bureau (BBB) in both your state and in the state of the company that is offering the medical billing opportunity to see if there are any negative reports filed on the company in question. It would also be good to check the BBB in the surrounding states of the company offering the product because common sense says they probably started selling there opportunity close to home first.

4. Ask for and check any references provided by the company. This could get iffy because companies have been known to pay people to give a favorable report. Nonetheless, checking will give you the feeling that you did all you could to protect yourself and your investment instead of later feeling that you could have spared yourself if only you had checked.

5. Ask the company to mail you information concerning the opportunity. You will get a sense of the company just by the look of the materials they send you (if they send anything).

6. Visit billing forums or billing resource sites and post a message asking if anyone else has had any dealing with that company and how their experience was.

A medical billing opportunity is a package offered by a company that consists of:

a) **Training**-books and videos (sometime even 3 day seminars) that go over medical billing and why it's needed, the two type of billing services, how the medical billing process works, the use of the supplied billing software, clearinghouses and how to run a medical billing business.

b) **Software and Technical Support**- a choice of a claims only package or practice management package and a service package is given. The offering company could make the software or it is a reseller such as Medisoft Billing Software that is incorporated into the entire program.

c) **Marketing & Sales** (materials and advice)-books, videos, and marketing material that you will need to sell yourself and your company professionally. They usually have continuing website, fax and email support for new ideas to be passed along.

d) **Workshops**-from time to time, further training classes and update courses are offered to keep you abreast of any changes to the industry and marketplace.

These topics range in the amount of time spent, detail given, and the amount you're charged depending on the opportunity you chose.

Shopping around is the best thing you can do so you can make an informed choice depending on the level of billing experience and business knowledge you have.

Chapter 12

Where Do I Look For A Medical Billing Opportunity?

As always, here are a few business opportunity vendors that you can research and contact:

Company & Website	Phone Number
Claims Transit www.ambanet.net/info.htm	(580) 622-5809
Synergy MIS www.synergymis.com/	(800) 652-3500
ClaimTek www.claimtek.com	(800) 224-7450

Company & Website	Phone Number
Pacific Medical www.pacificmedical.com	(800) 815-6334
Medical Billing Business Resources www.medicalbillingbusinessres ources.com/	(865) 286-9124 (Ext.# 13)

Once again, I am not endorsing any of these medical billing opportunities I am just telling you which ones are known to be reputable in supporting the medical billing industry.

Chapter 13

What Is a Clearinghouse and How Does It Apply To Billing Services?

The way I like to describe this is to first have you visualize a few things:

1. There are hundreds of medical billing software vendors and they make their software in different ways called formats.

2. There are hundreds of insurance carriers that accept electronic submission of claims but they only accept claims sent in a certain format that their machines are able to read.

3. There is no standardized format that is universally used by either software vendors or insurance carriers to be able to send and receive information regardless of what kind of billing software you have (there are those governing forces that are trying to come up with one so that things would become easier for all, but that will take a while).

Until that time arrives there are several companies called "clearinghouses" that (for a fee) will accept the transmission of your claims regardless of what format that your billing software encrypts them in. These clearinghouses are contracted (for a fee) with certain insurance companies to translate the claims you send to them and reformat those claims to be forwarded to the proper insurance carrier in the format that they will accept.

Be sure that you contract with a clearinghouse that is contracted with several insurance carriers (called Payors) to ensure that your claims will be handled electronically from beginning to end.

I say that because if you send a claim to a clearinghouse and the insurance company that the claims are going to doesn't accept or is not contracted to accept claims from the clearinghouse they (the clearinghouse) will have to print the appropriate claim form and send it via mail (this is called dropping the claim to paper). You will be charged an extra fee if the clearinghouse has to drop a claim to paper.

One of the good things is that a clearinghouse will perform an error check on each claim to make sure that all the appropriate boxes on a claim are filled (this is not to say that if you fill a box with incorrect information such as the wrong procedure code in the correct box that they will catch it). Once you submit all the claims for a particular day at the same time to the clearinghouse (called a batch transmission) and all the information is checked the clearinghouse will send you a confirmation (called a transmittal report) to verify the amount of claims sent as a receipt.

Some software vendors will sell you an add-on to your billing software (called modules) that will allow you to send your claims directly to certain insurance carries such as Medicare, BC/BS, etc.. My suggestion is if you are new to the billing process that you wait before sending claims directly because you will not have the added safeguard of having your claims error checked before submission (once you understand the process and are confident about your skills you can purchase the modules in order to bypass the fees charged by the clearinghouse to transmit them for you).

Remember that just as we are in business and the level of services we provide are different the same goes for clearinghouses. Shop around for the clearinghouse that best fits your needs and budget but **DO NOT** choose one strictly because of your budget.

Take into consideration the level of customer service you will receive if you have problems (which you will) because if you have to wait due to customer service issues on behalf of your clearinghouse you could be losing money, creditability, and clients (hell, your time is valuable so don't let anyone or anything personal or business wise waste it).

Lastly, pay attention to the startup/enrollment fees that you will have to pay for each practitioner/practice you will be billing for (the clearinghouse I deal with charged a set fee regardless of how many practitioners/practices I bill for).

Chapter 14

How Do Clearinghouses Charge?

Here is an example of the pricing from one of the clearinghouse vendors:

Description of Service	Pricing
One-time Enrollment Fee: (charge to enroll your service with the clearinghouse/the charge to enroll each practice or practitioner you will be billing for)	Waived and $125/Practice
Commercial Insurance Claims: (all insurance companies besides Medicare, Medicaid, Blue Cross Blue Shield, and GHI of NY)	$.39 per claim

Description of Service	Pricing
Non Commercial Claims: (Medicare, Medicaid, Blue Cross Blue Shield, and GHI of NY)	$.39 per claim
Printed Claims: (claims dropped to paper)	$.45 per claim
Patient Statements:	Not Applicable
Eligibility/Referrals:	Not Applicable
Payers: (the amount of insurance companies that the clearinghouse is contracted with)	900
Transmission: (the way you send claims to the clearinghouse	Modem/Cable/T1-3

Chapter 15

Which Clearinghouse Should I Use?

Company & Website	Phone Number
Claimsnet.com www.claimsnet.com	(800) 356-1511
DataClaim www.dataclaim.com	(888) 328-2252
ET&T Clearinghouse www.ettch.com	(480) 325-0901
Medi.com www.medi.com	(888) 334-6278
MedAvant www.medavanthealth.com	(800) 882-0802

Company & Website	Phone Number
NDC Health EDI Services www.ndchealth.com	(404) 728-2000
Texas Health Information www.thinedi.com	(972) 766-6730
Transmedic www.transmedic.com	(800) 795-6108
Emdeon Corporation www.emdeon.com	(877) 932-6301
Zirmed, Inc. www.zirmed.com	(877) 4-ZIRMED

Chapter 16

How Much Does It Cost To Start A Billing Service?

Despite what you may have seen or heard **You CANNOT start a medical billing company for just a few hundred dollars.** The average startup costs between $3000 - $5000. Your total expenses will be a little less than that depending on the amount of things you may already have (computer, chair, second phone line, etc.).

"Wow that's a lot of money! I saw a site that will get me started for about $500". That's what you're thinking right? Well let's look at the necessities you will need and the pricing involved (this is taking into consideration that you are starting from scratch):

Computer/Monitor/Modem = $1700 and up

Printer/Copier/Fax Machine/Scanner = $600 and up

Backup Devices (flash drives, zip drive, secondary hard drives, etc.) = $150 and up

Filing Cabinets = $125 and up

Hanging file Folders = $3.99 per box

Office Furniture and Accessories = $500 and up

Second Phone Line = $200

Postage (advertising, invoices) = $300 and up

Billing Software = $1200 and up

Technical Support = $400 and up

Accounting Software = $150 and up

Printer/fax/Copier Paper = $22 per carton and up

Forms (HCFA's, UB04's, ADA's) = $100 worth to use and to keep on hand

Disks (DVD, CD's) = $100 worth to use and to keep on hand

Books (ICD 9, CPT 4, HCPCS, etc.) = $180 and up

Consumables (toner, inks, ribbons) = $150 and up (depending on the machine it could be a lot lower but keep a supply on hand at all times)

Business Cards/Letterhead/Envelopes = $200 and up

The next thing I need to mention is the opening of a business account. You will need to contact either the bank you do business with now or shop around for the best services and rates with regard to business accounts.

Chapter 17

Why Do I Need To Set Up A Business Account?

Why do you need a business account? Simply put, separating your personal accounts and business accounts just makes good sense as well as it will be easier to track the progress of your business. Another reason is that banks do require a business account be opened if the payments you receive for your services will be in the name of your billing company.

When I first started I didn't have a business account set up and the doctors would write me checks in my business name and I was unable to cash them at the bank I had been doing business with for years.

This is how I found out the hard way that I had not set my business up correctly. The new business clerk, bless his soul set up an appointment with a friend who was a CPA up the block from the bank for me.

My partner and I visited him and he helped us understand what it meant to be in business, how to operate within the guidelines of the law, run and maintain our business and he didn't charge a penny for the info or getting us set up as a corporation (except for when he does our taxes). By the grace of GOD I was spared an ordeal that would have just gotten worse down the line.

As I said before, banks charge differently for their services and differ in the amount that they want you to start your business account with.

Because I bank with a very well known financial institution and I trust them implicitly I had to open my account with $5,000. This was yet another one of those unexpected expenditures that I was not counting on and couldn't see coming.

The good news is that once you pay for everything you need to get started your costs per month will be minimal compared to what you put out initially. I took about $6000 and loaded myself up with everything I might need to run this business including putting aside another $1000 strictly for advertising purposes. Be prepared to spend a lot when it comes down to your advertising because you are not really in business until you land that first client.

Getting the word out is the best thing you can do for yourself but don't overspend your budget (stickers, newspaper ads, banner advertising, sponsorships, etc.) on things you can't afford until you have a constant income stream. So altogether my initial start-up cost was $12,000 but if you do your homework, shop around, and align yourself with the right people you will not have to spend as much money as we did or fall into the same potholes.

Well, we have certainly come along way in our quest for the understanding of what medical billing is, can we make a living at it, and what we will spend in order to get started.

The next step is to pick out a business name, become some sort of legal entity, gather paperwork what will help you conduct business on a professional level, and all the other things that go into being in business.

So hang on, because when we are finished with the remaining questions you will be able to put into action what you have learned.

Chapter 18

How Should I Set Up My Business?

Before we get into the steps of setting up a business you should be aware that this is not my area of expertise. I strongly suggest that you consult with both an attorney and CPA to set up your business within the limits of the law in your county and state.

When I first thought about opening our billing service I asked questions of those individuals that already had services up and running. On the surface this seemed like the right thing to do but I never took into consideration that we were in different parts of the nation and the laws that applied to them didn't to me.

The next thing I came to realize was that some of the individuals were just "winging it" themselves and giving me advice that could potentially destroy my business and personal assets (bank accounts and home) if I were to be sued. That's right folks; you can be sued by a practitioner (for several reasons) or by a patient (if you conduct soft collections for a physician and in your zeal to collect owed funds you overstep your bounds in the eyes of the law).

I also asked questions about choosing a business name and was told that I could choose any name that I thought was fitting for my company.

As I said before I come from a corporate background and was aware that certain names were not going to give off the sense of professionalism that I would need to build a respectable business.

Nevertheless, I never thought that if by accident I were to choose a name that was already taken that I could be sued (worst case scenario) or instructed to change the name after I had already built a following, and spent hundreds in advertising and printing costs (letterhead, brochures, envelopes, etc.).

Then when I thought I had everything licked I was told that I might not be able to open a business in my apartment or in the particular part of the city where I lived.

You Got It, some counties regulate the location (zone) and type of business that you can run within that county. Not to mention some counties require that you register your business with them as well as the state you are doing business in.

I am not telling you all of these mishaps to try and discourage you but to reinforce what I have been saying since the beginning **"research everything and don't cut corners"**.

Take what others have to say with a grain of salt until you can substantiate what they are saying is a fact.

So please, please consult with an attorney, accountant, the Small Business Administration (SBA) and the Service Corps of Retired Executives (S.C.O.R.E) before you set out to set yourself up for failure.

Chapter 19

How Can I Protect My Business From Mistakes That Might Be Made?

The answer is, *"**Get Your Business Insured**"* (this is not to be taken lightly folks).

Naturally, no one expects to be sued, but as a small business owner, you could be. Clients rely on your knowledge to help them move their businesses forward, and you're liable for any mistakes you might make. As independent professionals began playing such a critical role in the economy, claims against them rose due to the exposure. So no matter how careful you are or how solid your client relationship is, it's better to be safe than sorry and purchase professional liability insurance.

Professional liability insurance (also known as Errors and Omissions or E&O insurance) provides protection against loss incurred by the insureds negligent act, error, or omission. If you're providing a professional service or rendering a professional opinion, this coverage is highly recommended. In fact, some physicians may even require that you have Professional Liability Insurance before hiring you.

You can find this form of insurance policy by calling a local insurance agent or banking institution.

Chapter 20

What Should I Name My Business?

One of the most important business decisions you will ever make is what to name your company, its products and services.

One of the first decisions you may need to make is whether your company name and service name should be the same. It depends upon the nature of your business but if the nature of your business demands that you have different names for your company- products or services, you should do the best you can to connect them together. For example:

Microsoft has done a great job doing this. The company name is almost always used in conjunction with every product name: Microsoft Windows, Microsoft Word, Microsoft Excel, Microsoft Office, etc.

Another way names are chosen is by associating your own name with the service you are offering which seems to work well if you are in the business of consulting or professional services. For example:

Paul's Medical Billing, P.G. Practice Mngt., or Hackett's Medical Management

Then, there's the NON-Name. These are names that have no dictionary meaning.

They can take on whatever meaning or image the company decides since they are not associated with any person, place or thing, in any language. For example:

Stelo Medical Management or Stelo Enterprises

The advantages are:

1. It's distinct; free and clear of competition

2. It's unlimited in language; free and clear of translation problems

3. It's proprietary; free and clear of restriction

4. It's descriptive

The disadvantage is:

1. I had to invest heavily in marketing in order to build a favorable, recognizable image for a name like this.

The main objective of a name is clarity, recognition, and individuality (that which makes you stand out

A Name Should:	A Name Should Not:
Be distinctive	Sounding like a competitor
Be descriptive	Using your own name
Be global	Adapting a local or regional name (Paul's East Coast Billing)
Be unique and creative	Sounding like every other business

A Name Should:	A Name Should Not:
Be memorable	Promoting a broad category (Healthcare Management)
Registered and protected	The use of initials
Be easy to say and spell	Being overly creative (being cute)

Look at your competitor's names within your industry (what images do they evoke and what messages do they convey?). Write down what you like and dislike and use the likes when brainstorming.

Brainstorm about a name that sounds pleasing to the ear, describes the service you will be providing, and think about how it would look when written (the design/logo/motto that will make it memorable).

Remember whom you will be marketing to and who else will be exposed to your name while marketing so be sensitive toward gender, race and religion.

Write down the advantages and disadvantages of the names you have chosen and pick only the top four. The next step is to take them on a test drive by asking others which name they would choose to do business with if they were looking for a biller.

I only tell you this because as humans we are partial when we create something and only an unbiased opinion will allow you to see through a potential customers eyes.

Chapter 21

How Do I Know I'm Picking a Unique Business Name?

Check for the availability, search for conflicts and or similarities. You don't want to name a business that can cause problems later, because it confuses you with some other business or worse.

There are several ways to check for the availability of a name and here are my top five suggestions:

1. See An Attorney. Using an attorney to conduct the search is very costly but it will be a complete search that you can count on. The average cost to search a name on a national basis is about $1,500, or about $30 per state (and doesn't include the cost for the lawyers time).

Companies spend $25,000 or more just to search a name globally. The cost to register a name with the U.S. Patent & Trademark Office also varies depending upon the nature of the application. Since you will probably talk to an attorney about other start-up matters, you should also ask them about how much they will charge to conduct a business name search.

Generally you want to first do your own check to catch any obvious conflicts.

2. The fastest and simplest way to start researching a name is to do an Internet search. Use the top search engines (Yahoo, AOL, Lycos, Google, MSN, Alta Vista, etc.) and see whether or not the name you are considering isn't already being used by someone else.

3. Check with the **U.S. Patent and Trademark Office** website at www.uspto.gov.

4. Check using other websites like **Knowx** at www.knowx.com or **Dunn & Bradstreet** at sbs.dnb.com.

If you are going to put your business online it would be best to check if the name you have chosen (or domain name as it is know on the net) is free and clear to use. Here are a few:

Company & Website

Network Solutions
www.networksolutions.com/cgi-bin/whois/whois

Go Daddy
http://www.godaddy.com/

Register
http://www.register.com/

Name Cheap
http://www.namecheap.com/

Verisign
www.verisign.com/domain-name-services/index.html

Chapter 22

Will The Name I Choose Be Exclusive To My Company?

You can't reserve a business name completely nor can you have exclusive use of it. This is the most common misunderstanding about business names.

A business name is a lot like a personal name. The first named Paul Hackett cannot claim exclusive use of that name and he can't make all the other Paul Hackett's in the world change their names. The same applies to business names.

Wendy's can't make Wendy's Hardware Store change its name, and Wendy's Hardware Store in Manhattan can't sue Wendy's Hardware Store in San Francisco.

However, just as you have rights to your own identity, so does your company. One Paul Hackett can sue another Paul Hackett for using his identity, having bills sent to the wrong address, or purposely confusing people. For example:

McDonald's can sue just about anybody trying to use the McDonald's name for a business selling fast foods.

The confusion starts because business names are registered by different authorities in different places, and on different levels:

1. The first and simplest business name is your own name, which might be enough for Paul G. Hackett using Hackett's Medical Billing. This kind of business name normally requires no additional paperwork, although most business owners end up registering a name anyhow to establish their legal claim to it.

2. The second normal common level of business names is called DBA (for doing business as) or Fictitious Business Name, which gives an individual the right to operate under a business name with signs, bank accounts, checks, and so on. These are generally registered and legalized by county governments within states.

There might be a Hackett's Medical Billing as a DBA in many counties within a given state, and across many different states. To register a business with a fictitious business name, first call your county clerk's office for details. Then you will have to visit the county clerk, pay a fee of less than $100, and do some legal advertising using forms you can fill out while there.

3. The third level is the corporation (S Corporations, C Corporations, or LLC's). Corporations are registered at the state level and only one can have the same name in the same state. However, there is no guarantee that there won't be many businesses registered as Hackett's Medical Billing in several counties in a state, and a corporation registered as Hackett's Medical Billing Corporation. This kind of duplication happens.

To establish a corporation you can use a national services such as **www.incorporation.com**, have an attorney do it, or you can contact or write to the Department of State (division of corporations and state records) for details about applying for yourself.

Even though duplicate business names are very possible, and quite common, you do still have the right to protect and defend you own business name, once you've built the business around it.

In other words, McDonald's can and will sue anybody who starts a new restaurant named McDonald's serving any fast foods. When one business is confused with another, being first matters.

When somebody tries to establish a second Hackett's Medical Billing where it would confuse people with the first, then the first Hackett's Medical Billing has a legal right to prevent it.

If this were to go to court, the first one to use the name is likely to win, but if the first one sat quietly while the other one built the name, then there is more doubt.

An existing business should always watch out for people using the same or confusingly similar names, because the sooner it complains, the better for its legal arguments.

Chapter 23

What Should Be My Business Structure?

Your business structure alludes to the type of organization formula your company will follow. When opening a new business, you can't get away from deciding or choosing the structure of the business. Some of the factors that should influence your decisions include:

Legal restrictions

Liabilities assumed

Type of business operation

Earnings distribution

Capital needs

Number of employees

Tax advantages or disadvantages

Length of business operation

With that said, here is a brief description of each type of business organization. <u>Only an attorney or a CPA can advise you properly</u> on the advantages and disadvantages as they apply to your particular situation. **<u>So, Consult With Them !!!!</u>**

Sole Proprietorship

This is the easiest and least costly way of starting a business.

A sole proprietorship is formed by finding a location and opening the doors for business. There are likely to be fees to obtain business name registration, a fictitious name certificate and other necessary licenses.

Partnership

The two most common types of partnerships are general and limited. A general partnership can be formed simply by an oral agreement between two or more persons while a limited partnership places limitations on the length that the partnership will exist.

I suggest that if you are setting up a partnership that you sit down and detail all the titles, responsibilities of each partner, the limitation of each partners power within the partnership, and what will happen to a partners share if they were to die or become incapacitated.

You should then have a legal partnership agreement drawn up by an attorney because it will be helpful in solving any disputes (especially when partners are responsible for the other partner's business actions, as well as their own). For example:

If you and I were partners and I without your knowledge commit fraud (such as accepting kickbacks on behalf of the company) and CMS brings charges against me you will also be liable as a partner in the crime.

A Partnership Agreement should include the following:

Type of business.

Amount of equity invested by each partner.

Division of profit or loss.

Partner's compensation.

Distribution of assets on dissolution.

Duration of partnership.

Provisions for changes or dissolving the partnership.

Dispute settlement clause.

Restrictions of authority and expenditures.

Settlement in case of death or incapacitation.

Corporation

As mentioned before you may incorporate without an attorney, **but legal advice is highly recommended**. The corporate structure is usually the most complex and more costly to organize than the other two business formations. Control depends on stock ownership. Persons with the largest stock ownership, not the total number of shareholders, control the corporation.

With control of stock shares or 51 percent of stock, a person or group is able to make policy decisions. Control is exercised through regular board of directors' meetings and annual stockholders' meetings.

Records must be kept to document decisions made by the board of directors. Small, closely held corporations can operate more informally, but record keeping cannot be eliminated entirely.

Officers of a corporation can be liable to stockholders for improper actions. Liability is generally limited to stock ownership, except where fraud is involved. You may want to incorporate as a "C" or "S" corporation.

LLC (Limited Liability Company)

Be careful with this one, because the LLC's formation is different from state to state, with advantages in some states that aren't relevant in others.

An LLC is usually a lot like an S corporation with a combination of some limitations on legal liability and some favorable tax treatment for profits and transfer of assets. This is a newer form of legal entity, and often harder to establish than a corporation.

Why would you establish an LLC instead of a corporation? In general, the LLC has to be missing two of the four characteristics of a corporation (limited liability, centralized management, continuity of life, and free transferability of ownership interest) but **only a good local attorney with small business experience or a good CPA will be able to answer that question with regard to your particular situation**.

Chapter 24

What Is a Business Plan?

Answering this question can become very technical and over-whelming so I will simplify it by first giving you a definition of what a business plan is. Then I will give you an outline so you can get an understanding as to the planning that goes into one.

Definition

A business plan is a written outline that communicates the values, goals, marketing strategies, financial strategies and forecasts, competition analysis, and how the company will go about implementing all the above mentioned to make the company a success.

A business plan does two things:

1. It allows the owner to step back from the normal flow of operations and look at ways to develop and improve the business (kind of like being a bystander looking at your business where you will be able to see things you never noticed before because of being personally involved).

2. It will allow an individual with no prior knowledge of your industry to understand exactly what your industry is, who your competition is, what your market is like (is it a growth-stagnant- or declining market), why you are unique in this market, what

value your services will bring to this industry, the level of understanding that you have about the industry-market-and customer and how much potential profits your company could reap from conducting business in this market.

The second reason given above will be necessary if you try to get investors to generate monies for getting your business up and running or if you ask a bank for a business loan for the same reason.

No one that you don't know is going to part with their money and give it to you to start your business if you can't prove to them that you are an expert at medical billing, fully understand your market, that you understand how to run and maintain a business financially, and that your business will turn a sizable enough profit in order to make them more money than they originally put in.

A business plan depending on the type of business will differ in length, complexity and detail. It will change over time as your business gets off the ground, begins to generate an income, or there are changes in the market that affect you, the customer, and the industry (so, be prepared to update it periodically).

The following is an outline of a simple business plan. The subsections I have included will serve as a guide to help you in the drafting of it to make it a more manageable task:

Introduction

1. Give a detailed description of the business and its goals.

2. Discuss the ownership of the business and the legal structure.

3. List the skills and experience you bring to the business.

4. Identify your competitors

5. Discuss the advantages you and your business have over your competitors.

Marketing

1. Discuss the products/services offered.

2. Identify the customer demand for your product/service.

3. Identify your market, its size and locations.

4. Explain how your product/service will be advertised and marketed.

5. Explain the pricing strategy.

Financial Management

1. Explain your source and the amount of initial equity capital.

2. Develop a monthly operating budget for the first year.

3. Develop an expected return on investment and monthly cash flow for the first year.

4. Provide projected income statements and balance sheets for a two year period.

5. Discuss your break-even point.

6. Explain your personal balance sheet and method of compensation.

7. Discuss who will maintain your accounting records and how they will be kept.

Operations

1. Explain how the business will be managed on a day-to-day basis.

2. Discuss hiring and personnel procedures.

3. Discuss insurance, lease or rent agreements, and issues pertinent to your business.

4. Account for the equipment necessary to produce your products or assist your service.
5. Account for the production or delivery of your products or services.

Executive Summary

Summarize your business goals, objectives and express your commitment to the success of your business using all the parts mentioned above to back your statement up.

Chapter 25

Where Can I Go To Get Help Writing a Business Plan?

As usual, in this section I was going to give you an actual business plan used by a medical billing service so you could better identify with it since numbers and verbiage was included. After careful consideration I decided that it would benefit you more if I were to tell you where you can see it, reword it and print it instead of adding an extra 40 pages of fluff to this book.

To see a copy of an actual medical billing services business plan with the verbiage and figures included visit:

www.bplans.com/medical_billing_business_plan/executive_summary_fc.cfm

They will not allow you to edit the business plan anymore but at least you can see what one looks like. Trust me when I say that these types of plans including your marketing plan are complicated to put together so unless you have someone that has a great understanding of what they are doing then I suggest that you purchase some software that will help you do it in an easy to follow format.

As I said before there are many types and lengths of business plans and they are forever changing along with your business. If you find that you need help articulating your vision or don't know exactly where in the business plan it should be discussed then visit the professionals:

The Small Business Administration

www.sbaonline.sba.gov

Or

Service Corps Of Retired Executives

www.score.org

Regardless of what you are trying to do business wise there are several people at either location that will be willing to assist you. I go there for advice on everything instead of asking our lawyer or CPA and wasting money on the simpler questions.

The second benefit to you is that the majority of those people have hands on experience in setting up a business, legal issues, applying for grants and loans, setting up IPO's (Initial Public Offerings), getting investors, marketing, sales and whatever else you can think of. The best thing is they enjoy helping others become as successful (if not more successful) than they have become.

Chapter 26

What Is Compliance and Do I Need To Be Compliant?

Compliance is a dynamic process that helps to ensure billing companies, physicians, hospitals, nursing homes and those entities that support healthcare services are better able to fulfill their commitment to ethical behavior and to meet the changes and challenges being imposed upon them by Congress, OIG (Office of the Inspector General), GAO (General Accounting Office), HHS (Health and Human Services), DOH (Department Of Health) and both federal and private insurers.

Ultimately, OIG hopes that a voluntarily created compliance program will enable billing companies, physicians, hospitals, and those entities that support healthcare services to meet their goals and substantially reduce fraud, waste and abuse, as well as the cost of health care to Federal, State and private health insurers.

Do you need to be compliant?

YES, absolutely! Here are the first 5 reasons that come to my mind when asked this question:

1. You want to protect your new business from any mishaps on behalf of a practitioner, another vendor, or your own mistakes.

2. If the government is stressing healthcare providers to create and implement a compliance plan why would they or should they do business with a company that is not also diligent enough to educate and protect themselves.

3. Later on you will use the plan as a marketing strategy (benefits) to sell yourself to a prospective client (in-person, by brochure, or sales letter).

4. OIG has made it clear that if they are investigating a company and that company has a compliance program in effect and they are actively trying to educate their personnel that they (OIG) will show leniency on behalf of that company or practice.

5. It also gives you and your staff a set of rules to live by. The plan will clearly state how everyone (including management and owners) are to act with respect:

To each other,

Your role in your function,

List who your compliance officer is and how they can be con-acted in case any of the rules are broken or if one thinks that they were broken,

Confidentiality,

Fraud and abuse,

Proper coding practices,

Phone etiquette,

Consequences of ones actions and

The degrees and extent of disciplinary actions

Chapter 27

What are The Components Of a Compliance Program?

Government investigations into physician billing has focused on four areas:

1. Upcoding

2. Unbundling

3. Unnecessary services

4. Unperformed services.

Healthcare fraud is a problem for all types and sizes of providers, billing companies, hospitals, nursing homes, and healthcare vendors. Fraud includes false or improper reimbursement of claims, unlawful physician incentive plans, kickbacks, unlawful referral practices, and the failure to adequately assure compliance.

CMS (Center for Medicare and Medicaid Services) and OIG have implemented extensive policies aimed at eliminating fraudulent billing. There are seven elements for an effective compliance program and here they are:

1. Implementing written policies, procedures, and standard of conduct.

2. Designating a compliance officer and compliance committee.

3. Conducting effective training and education.

4. Developing effective lines of communication.

5. Enforcing standards through well-publicized disciplinary guidelines and developing policies addressing dealings with sanctioned individuals.

6. Conducting internal monitoring and auditing.

7. Responding promptly to detected offenses, developing corrective action, and reporting to the government.

As before if I were to break down each part it would take up almost another 20 pages so visit the following regulatory website for keeping up-to-date on all issues healthcare related:

cms.hhs.gov

Chapter 28

What Kind Of Contracts &Paperwork Will I Need When Signing A Doctor?

What I find alarming is the fact that people ask me this question before they ask "What Questions Should I Ask A Practitioner?" considering that they will never get to the signing stage if the initial interview is not conducted in a professional manner. At the same time I understand that in our quest to sign a doctor so we can start earning money we tend to forget about the in between steps <u>we have to take</u> to get to that point.

So before I answer the question in the topic I feel the need to address what you should be initially speaking about with a doctor on the phone or in person.

The questions in figure 1 and 2 will help you to develop your talk track so you can move a conversation along smoothly and get the vital information you will need to assess the practitioner's current situation. As you go over them think about the questions that you may be asked by a practitioner (how you run your business, how will you get the claims, how do you handle discrepancies, etc.) and how you will answer them quickly and intelligently to gain their trust in you and your company.

This is important because being new you have no references to back up how well you conduct business so the way you present your company with the professional looking material you submit, your knowledge of the market and industry, your background and experience, and your communication skills is critical.

After that I will refocus on the question in the topic, answer it and give you two examples of contracts (figure 3 and 4) to get you familiar with them.

I will also give you examples of other forms that you can copy onto your letterhead to get you started. You can get more forms and different versions of forms from billing resource websites and from billing forums by posting messages asking for them. If you are a paid member of any of these sites you will have access to these forms as well as sales materials you can use to attract clients without having become a copywriter overnight.

You will also, need to research medical forms companies or business stationary stores to get your CMS-1500's and UB-04's.

Remember three things:

1. No one form is etched in stone (except the CMS-1500, UB-04, and ADA forms), you can choose which ones work best for you and your clients.

2. Most of your clients will have their own forms (except the CMS-1500, UB-04, and ADA forms) that they are accustomed to using and will not want to change so ask for copies of them and keep them on hand.

3. When it comes to contracts **always make sure you have them looked over or prepared by a lawyer** before you use them. **Only a lawyer** will be able to tell you if a contract is worded correctly, is valid to use, and if it is enough to cover your business within the eyes of the law if a dispute should arise.

Figure 1

**Questions To Ask Prospective Practitioners When They
Call To Inquire About Your Services**

1. Are you a group or solo practice?   (If solo, skip to question 3

2. How many doctors are in your practice?

3. What is your specialty?

4. Where is your practice located?

5. Is this the address you will be using to receive payments?

6. Do you currently have a billing staff or do you outsource?

(Depending on their answer go directly to the appropriate section that follows)

If They Have A Billing Staff

1. How many billing employees do you have?

2. How many hours per week is spent by your biller(s) processing claims? What is their average hourly pay?

3. How many claims on average per month do you process?

4. Do you process any no-fault or workman's comp. claims? What percentage of each?

5. What is the average dollar amount billed per month? What is your turn around time like?

6. What is your percentage of rejected and unpaid claims? Do you appeal all of your denied claims? What is your success rate on getting paid on denied claims?

7. Well, now that I know a little about your practice, why are you interested in outsourcing your billing?

8. Will you want us to submit your claims only or do you need us to follow-up and post payments too? Do you want us to take over the entire operation (full practice management)?

9. Are there any questions you would like to ask me?

10. Have I answered all of your questions and addressed all of your concerns?

11. Will you rather to be charged on a per claim basis or on a percentage of the monthly amount collected?

12. When are you looking for (your business name) to start processing your claims?

13. I can come by on (pick the day) at (pick the time) for you to fill out the necessary paperwork or would (pick the next day) at (pick the time) be better for you?

If They Outsource

1. Who is currently process your claims?

2. What kind of service are they doing for you (submission only or submission-follow-up & posting of payments)?

3. Is there anything special that they are doing for you that you will also want us to fulfill?

4. How are you getting them your patient data (mail, fax, pick-up)?

5. What is your turnaround time?

6. What is your rejected claim percentage? Denied claims percentage? Are appeals conducted on all denied claims? What is the percentage of successful denial payment?

7. How many claims on average per month do you process?

8. What is the average dollar amount billed per month?

6. What is your rejected claim percentage? Denied claims percentage? Are appeals conducted on all denied claims? What is the percentage of successful denial payment?

7. How many claims on average per month do you process?

8. What is the average dollar amount billed per month?

9. How much do you pay per claim? Or what percentage are you paying per month?

10. Well, now that I know a little about your practice, why are you interested in changing companies?

11. Are there any questions you would like to ask me?

12. Have I answered all of your questions and addressed all of your concerns?

13. Will you want to be charged by the same method (per claim, percentage) you are using now?

14. When will you be looking for (the name of your company) to start processing your claims?

15. I can come by on (pick the day) at (pick the time) for you to fill out the necessary paperwork or would (pick the next day) at (pick the time) be better for you?

Figure 2

Detailed Provider Profile Sheet

(Questions to ask in a face-to-face setting)

Date: _____

Practice Name: _____

Specialty: _____

Provider Name: _____

Specialty: _____

Specialty: _____

Specialty: _____

Office Manager: _____

Address:

_____

_____

_____

1. Do you currently have a computer? ☐Yes ☐ No
If yes, what software program do you use?

2. How many insurance claims do you process per month?

3. What is the average dollar amount per claim?

4.   How long on average does it take to receive payment?
Less than 20 days   ☐21-30 days   31-40 days   ☐ 41-50 days
☐ 51-60 days   ☐ 61-70 days   ☐ Over 70 days

5. What percentage of your claims is returned for correction?

6. Do you enter your claims on your computer, print and mail them?   ☐ Yes ☐ No

7. What percentage of your claims are:
Medicare _____%   Medicaid _____% BC/BS _____%
GHI _____%   W/Comp _____%

8. What other insurance companies do you participate in?

9. Do you file claims electronically to the carrier?   Yes ☐ No

10. Do you have any insurance carrier that is more difficult to obtain payment from than others? Yes No If yes, state name.

11. Do you have personnel devoted totally to claims processing?

12. How much time is spent on claims processing?

13. How much time is spent on claims follow up?

14. If you could change the way your practice processes and files it's claims, what changes would you make?

16. Have you ever considered an outside billing service before? Yes ☐ No If yes, why haven't you contracted with them?

17. If you were shown a way that you could do the majority of your claims electronically, without changing your daily routine in the office, would you be interested in hearing more about it?

Now, your potential client should begin asking you about how much you will charge them to deliver your services. So using the information that you just recorded above refer to your pricing structure and that is where negotiations begin.

If you do well your potential client will ask to see your contract so here are two samples. If you find that you client is still reluctant use the trial contact in figure 3 and if they are willing to sign a long term contract use figure 4.

Figure 3

<u>These contracts are ONLY samples and should be rewritten with the assistance of a business attorney!</u>

30 Day Trial Agreement For Electronic Claims Submission

This agreement is between _____

(herein called "Billing Center") and

_____

(herein called "Provider").

Whereas, both parties wish to enter into a 30 Day Trial Agreement. Billing Center offers electronic medical claims processing services in the healthcare industry and wishes to evaluate the service requirements and need of the Provider. The Provider wishes to realize and increase savings and efficiency by the use of the Billing Centers electronic medical claims processing and evaluate the service provided over a 30 day period.
Therefore, both parties hereto agree to the following:

1. Billing Center will pick up Superbill from Provider on_____, unless other arrangements have been made and both parties agree.

2. Billing Center agrees that any information learned regarding Providers patients or business would be held strictly confidential.

3. Provider shall pay an initial setup fee of $150.00, upon completion of this agreement, provided that they choose to continue utilizing services of Billing Center.

4. Provider agrees to pay Billing Center_____dollars ($_____), per claim submitted during the trial period. Billing Center will invoice provider on the first business day of the new month and attach to the invoice a confirmation report from the respective insurance companies of claims submitted. Payment is due in full within seven (7) days.

5. In the event, the Provider wishes to process any prior rejected or denied claims for payment, Provider agrees to pay three dollars and fifty cents ($3.50) for each appeal conducted on a denied claim. A charge of two dollars and fifty cents ($2.50) for the resubmission of rejected claims if due Provider error.

6. At the end of the 30 Day Trail Period, both parties will meet to discuss required services, customized reports and the ongoing cost of the Billing Center service. In the event, that the billing service is not granted or scheduled an appointment to discuss their services within a seven-day period the Provider will be held responsible and invoiced $150.00 (#3) and costs pertaining to (#4). Provider acknowledges that the cost of service may increase after the said 30 days of evaluation.

Also, at the end of this agreement, providing that both parties agree to the future cost of service, they will enter into a (1) year service agreement customized to the Provider's needs and requirements.

7. Limitation of Liability: The Provider agrees to maintain copies of all patient information supplied to the Billing Center so that at no time will the Billing Center process data that is not simultaneously maintained in the Providers own office.

The Billing Center also agrees to use its best efforts to maintain a high professional standard in the execution of its services so as to minimize any errors, damages and/ or loss of Provider data during the submission process. To this degree, the Billing Center has no liability to the Provider if any of all data is lost, stolen, and/ or destroyed by any means.

The Provider agrees that all information supplied to the Billing Center is true and accurate to the best of the Providers knowledge. Furthermore, the Provider also agrees to hold the Billing Center harmless from any liability resulting form violations of City, State and/ or Federal regulations to the collection of the Provider's insurance claims or account receivables. In the event that the Billing Center should require the aid in defense for any such proceedings, the Provider agrees to absorb the costs associated from pending litigation.

This 30 Day Trial agreement is made this:

_____ day of _____, 200____

_____   _____
Physician or Principal   **Billing Center's Authorized**
                                                           Signer

Figure 4

Billing Service Acquisition Agreement

The service agreement is made this _____day of

_____, 200___, by and between Stelo Medical
Management, Inc., (hereinafter called "Billing Center") and

_____,
(hereinafter called "Provider"). The Billing Center and Provider
agree to mutually enter this agreement for a period of one year
(12 months).

Whereas, Billing Center offers the service of processing
insurance claims for Providers, and whereas Provider is desirous
of using the services provided by the Billing Center, the parties
hereby agree as follows:

1. **Services:** Billing Center herein agrees to process Provider
claims only after they have been edited and error corrected, either
by the Billing Centers own editing software or a competent
clearing house. The Billing Center will collect claims data
information in the form of patient encounters/superbills once per
week, either by facsimile transmission, physical pick up or mail,
on the day agreed upon by both parties.

Claims will be processed and submitted within (1) business day
of collection, with the exception of those claims containing
errors, which will be referred back to the Provider for necessary
corrections.

2. **Patient Data:** The Provider will fax or mail the patient demographics, encounter form/superbills, and the front and back of the patients insurance card to the Billing Center for electronic submission once a week on _____.

3. **Charges:** The charge for the above mentioned service is $_____ **per claim.**

4. **Practice Management Package:** The Billing Center herein agrees to review, enter, error check, submit, check EOB's, post payments, generate accounts receivable statements, aging reports, conduct soft collections, send birthday-holiday-and thank you cards on behalf of the Provider.

5. **Charges:** The flat fee monthly charge for the above mentioned service is $_____. The Provider also has the option of paying $_____ **per claim** or _____ **percent** (_____%) of the amount collected by the Billing Center during that month.

6. **Individualized Services Conducted:** Additional charges will be applied for appeals, resubmitted claims, aging reports, financial reports, collection letters, and birthday-holiday-and thank you cards sent by the Billing Center but not covered under the agreed upon pricing plan. The above services will be invoiced in accordance to the Billing Centers pricing schedule per item processed or sent.

7. **Invoices:** The Billing Center will invoice the Provider for all services performed during the proceeding billing period on a monthly basis.

Payment is due within ten (10) days following the date of billing. Invoices unpaid thirty (30) days after issuance of invoice will be subject to late charges of 1.5% per each month a balance is unpaid.

8.   **Limitation of Liability:** The Provider agrees to maintain copies of all patient information supplied to the Billing Center so that at no time will the Billing Center process data that is not simultaneously maintained in the Providers own office. The Billing Center also agrees to use its best efforts to maintain a high professional standard in the execution of its services so as to minimize any errors, damage and/or loss of Provider data during the submission process. To this degree, the Billing Center has no liability to the Provider if any or all data is lost, stolen, and/or destroyed by any means. The Provider agrees that all information supplied to the Billing Center is true and accurate to the best of the Providers knowledge. Furthermore, the Provider also agrees to hold the Billing Center harmless from any liability resulting from healthcare violations (e.g. fraudulent billing practices, inaccurate procedure/diagnosis coding, incorrect POS/DOS, or services not rendered, etc.) of City, State and/or Federal regulations to the collection of the Provider's insurance claims or account receivables. In the event that the Billing Center should require legal aid in defense for any such proceedings, the Provider agrees to absorb the costs associated with litigation.

9. **Termination:** The Provider after giving sixty (60) days prior written notice to the Billing Center may terminate the service agreement, with just cause only. However, the Billing Center may terminate this agreement without advanced notice after

receiving written notification of cancellation of any current contract. Upon termination of this agreement by either party, the Provider agrees to pay all outstanding charges within 10 days of the final termination date.

10. **Monthly Fees:** In the event that, less than ten (10) claims are processed in any given month, a penalty of $75.00 will be assessed to cover miscellaneous processing expenses. Should the Billing Center process and submit more than ten (10) claims per month, whether electronic or paper filings, this monthly fee will be waived with an exception to any other fees agreed upon.

11. **Setup Fees:** The Billing Center will waive all setup fees. The set up time with (your clearinghouse) is approximately seven weeks during which time Stelo will drop your claims to paper and submit them to the appropriate carriers. Once (your clearinghouse) has completed the set up procedure the Provider should receive payment between 7-21 days form the submission date of the Billing Center.

Billing Centers Acceptance   **Providers Acceptance**

_____   _____
Authorized Signature &   Authorized Signature &
          Title   Title

Figure 5

This is an example of all the info you will need from your client so you can save it into your medical billing software for when you actually begin billing for them:

CLIENT REGISTRATION FORM   (Used to get all of the practitioner ID #'s, U Pin #'s, and which insurance companies they participate in)
Practice Name:
Site#:
Address:
City, St, Zip:
Phone Number:
Fax Number:
Contact Names:

Specialty:
2 Digit Specialty Code:
Tax ID Number Employer Identification Number or Social Security Number:
License #:
UPIN #:
Individual Provider #'s:
Group Provider #:
Insurance Company's Contracted With:

Figure 6

Current Office Cost Analysis
(The Cost of Collection percentage is used to quantify the cost to have medical billing performed internally).

1. **The cost of Billing Staff on a monthly basis:**
a.) The cost of the Billing Staff:

Formula:
Hours Worked per Week **X** Hourly Wages **= Monthly Billing Staff Cost (M.B.S.C.)**

b.) The cost of Supervisory: The cost of Supervisory staff expenses has been calculated to be approximately 20% of the doctor's staff expenses for one month, for which goes toward such items as:
Employee benefits
Misc. Federal taxes
And many other staff expenses

Formula:
(M.B.S.C. **X** 20 %) + M.B.S.C. = **Total Monthly Staff Expenses**

2. **Monthly Office Hardgood and Softgood costs:** The average range is $500 to $800 per month, for a single doctor practice. This would include such items as:
Computers
Fax Machines
Copier Machines
Printers
Scanners

Consumables for Office Machines (cartridges, inks, ribbons, etc.)
And many other office needs (furniture, pens, whiteout, paper, forms, etc.)

Formula:
Total Monthly Staff Expenses + Monthly Office Costs = **Total Monthly Expenses**

3. **Monthly Gross Revenues:** This is denoted by the amount of money deposited each month
from collections on insurance claims and patient billing.

Formula:
Total Monthly Expenditures / Monthly Gross Revenue X 100

OR

$$\frac{\#2}{\#3}\,_{(100)} = \textbf{Cost of Collection Percentage}$$

NOTE: There are several different cost analysis calculators that can be used. My CFO came up with this simplistic form that anyone from my company (especially if they are in front of a client) will be able to use to show the physician a numeric value of how much he/she is spending on a monthly basis to process their claims.

I do suggest that you go to some of the billing forums and ask other billers how they quantify how much a doctor is spending and what kind of formulas and forms they use to calculate it. This way you can choose exactly which one is more to your liking (I'll say it again- research and creativity are the best tools you have at your disposal in your quest of becoming successful, so do it often).

Figure 7

Insurance Follow-Up Telephone Call Checklist
(Used when contacting insurance carriers in regard to claims)

Patient's name:_____

Policy
number:_____

Insurance carrier:_____

Account number:_____

Name of person with whom you spoke:_____

Was a claim received? ☐ Yes ☐ No   If so, when? _____

When will be claimed be processed?_____

Payment will be sent on: _____

Payment will be sent to:_____

What is the payment amount?_____

Insurance coverage was denied or charges reduced because:
_____
_____

What is the reduced charge?_____

Other comments or remarks:
_____
_____

Figure 8

Request For Additional Information

(Used to get missing info from physicians office regarding claims)

Claims Administrator:_____   Date Sent: ___/ ___/ ___

Doctor:_____,

While processing the claim referenced below, we find we are missing some information necessary to accurately file the claim. To minimize delays in the processing of this claim, please provide us with the requested information and return this form to us at (***) ***-**** as soon as possible. Please contact us if you have any questions. Thank you for your assistance.

Patient's Name: _____ _____

Date of Service: _____/ _____/ _____

Patient's Health Insurance Claim Number ____	Primary/Secondary Policy Info ____
Patient's Social Security Number ____	P.O.S vs. Procedure ____

Patient's Name, Sex & Date of Birth ____	Procedure Code ____
Patients Address/Correct Address ____	Diagnosis Code ____
Insureds Name, Sex & Date of Birth ____	Days or Units ____
Insureds Address ____	Charges ____
Policy Number ____	Explanation of Medical Benefits ____
Authorization Number ____	Blank Claim Sent ____
Provider/Network Identification Number ____	Approved/ Paid Amounts ____
Name of Referring Physician ____	Patient's Medigap # or Other Insurance # ____

Other: _____

Date Received From Doctor or Medical Office Personnel:
_____/ _____/ _____

Figure 9

OFFICE NOTES REQUEST
(Used to get vital information that may need to be sent to the
insurance carrier in order to back up a claims medical necessity
that was not originally attached)

To Whom It May Concern:
Attached are the office notes you requested for the following
patient and dates of service.

Patient:_____

ID#:_____

Date Of Service #:____ / _____ / _____

_____

_____

_____

_____

If you have any questions, please feel free to contact me at (***)
-*.

Sincerely,

Figure 10

APPEAL LETTER
(Used to appeal the findings of a claim that got denied)

Date: _____ / _____ / _____

Insurance Company: _____

Insured: _____

Patient:_____

D.O.B:_____

Insureds ID#_____

Date Of Service: _____ / _____ / _____

Provider:_____

Provider ID#:_____

To Whom It May Concern:

A claim was filed and denied for the above mentioned patient and date of service.

Our office is appealing this claim due to the reasons stated below:

_____
_____
_____

_____

_____

_____

_____

_____

_____

The initial claim along with copies of the denial, office notes, and attachments are enclosed to substantiate this appeal.

If you have any questions or need additional information, please contact me at
(***) ***-****.

Thank you for your prompt attention and cooperation in this matter.

Sincerely,

Figure 11

REQUEST FOR EXPLANATION OF BENEFIT'S

(Used to get EOB's from the physician's office so you post
payments and adjust the practices finances)

Date: _____/ _____/ _____

Dear Dr._____,

We have been informed by (insurance company) that payment
has been made and sent to your office. Unfortunately, we have
not received a copy of the EOB to post payment to your accounts
receivables. In our attempt to keep your A/R up to date we
would appreciate it if you could supply us with the following
EOB:

PATIENT: _____

DATE OF SERVICE:_____

INS CO.:_____

ID #: _____

Please fax the requested information to (***) ***-**** so that
we may rectify this matter in a timely fashion. If you have any
questions please feel free to contact me at (***) ***-****.

Sincerely,

Figure 12

Patient Bill

(This is for viewing only. Your billing software should allow you
to print one or you can print one from your accounting software)

RESPONSIBLE PARTY NAME /ADDRESS:

P. DITTY
168 AVENUE
ANYTOWN, NY 11411

PLEASE REMIT YOUR PAYMENT TO:

WOMEN'S HEALTH
51-24 98TH STREET
BOX 1521
NEW YORK, NY 10029
(***) ***-****

BILL DUE DATE: ____ / ____ / ____

ACCOUNT NO. : _____

AMOUNT ENCLOSED: $_____

**PLEASE REMOVE AND RETURN THE ABOVE PORTION
WITH YOUR PAYMENT.**

Physician: **C. Krause MD.**

Date Of Service	Description Of Service	Amount
PREVIOUS BALANCE		20.00
12/01/10	OFFICE/OUTPATIENT VISIT, EST, MOD	85.00
12/01/10	TRANS ECHO EXAM	420.00
12/01/10	MEDRXYPROGESTER ACETATE, 150MG	50.00
12/06/10	INSURANCE PAYMENT	(550.00)

Payment Due: 12/ 23 /10	Total Amount Due: $25.00
Patient's Name: Ms. P.-DITTY	Account Number: 1234567

Make Check Payable To → Woman's Health, Inc.

(INCLUDE ACCOUNT NUMBER ON YOUR CHECK)

Payments Received After The Payment Due Date Will Appear
On Your Next Statement

Figure 13

PLACE OF SERVICE CODES (POS)
(This is a quick reference guide for you.)

11 **Office**
12 **Home**
21 **Inpatient Hospital**
22 **Outpatient Hospital**
23 **Emergency Room - Hospital**
24 **Ambulatory Surgical Center**
25 **Birthing Center**
26 **Military Treatment Facility**
31 **Skilled Nursing Facility**
32 **Nursing Facility**
33 **Custodial Care Facility**
34 **Hospice**
41 **Ambulance (Land)**
42 **Ambulance (Air or Water)**
50 **Federally Qualified Health Center**
51 **Inpatient Psychiatric Facility**
52 **Psychiatric Facility - Partial Hospitalization**
53 **Community Mental Health Center**
54 **Intermediate Care Facility - Mentally Retarded**
55 **Residential Substance Abuse Treatment Facility**
56 **Psychiatric Residential Treatment Center**
60 **Mass Immunization Center**
61 **Comprehensive Inpatient Rehabilitation Facility**
62 **Comprehensive Outpatient Rehabilitation Facility**
65 **End Stage Renal Disease Treatment Facility**
71 **State or Local Public Health Clinic**
72 **Rural Heath Clinic**
81 **Independent Laboratory**
99 **Other Unlisted Facilities**

Figure 14

Fax Transmittal

Your Name
Your Title
Corporate Offices: (***) ***-****   Or   **Personal Cell**: (***) ***-****

If there is any problem with transmission, please contact the numbers above.

To: _____

Company: _____

Telephone Number: _____

Fax Number: _____

Number of Pages

_____

Date

_____

Comments:

Figure 15

You have heard me mention superbills/encounter forms so here's what one looks like. This is the form that you will receive from your doctors for each and every patient that you will need to bill for. The information is then taken from this form and you input it into the appropriate boxes in your medical billing software.

Once you input all the info for each patient, for that physician, for that practice then you use your software to compile all the info by insurance company (called batch or batching). Then you electronically submit those batches to the appropriate insurance company to be processed for payment.

Every practice uses different forms and templates so this is nowhere near the only format of superbill that you will come in contact with. Your software may also have the ability to create and customize these forms specifically for your clients practice and specialty. However, you don't have to stress yourself out creating these forms because your client is probably using a superbill/patient encounter/daysheet that they are comfortable with for their office (get a copy of their superbill, scan it, and change it when you need to).

Psychiatric Superbill

Providers Name:_____

Patient: _____

POS:_____   OT-PT: _____   DOS: _____

D.O.B:____ / ____ / _____   IN-PT _____   UR-HM: _____

DX: _____

ADMITTION DATE (In-Pt Only): ____/ ____/ _____

REF. PHYSICIAN: _____

[ ] COMMERCIAL INSURANCE [ ] PPO [ ] HMO [ ] MEDICARE [ ] OTHER

CPT CODE	DESCRIPTION	AMNT
90801	PSYCHIATRIC DIAGNOSTIC INTERVIEW	$100.00
90846	FAMILY PSYCHOTHERAPY (WITHOUT PATIENT)	$101.00
90847	FAMILY PSYCHOTHERAPY (CONJOINT)	$102.00
90853	GROUP PSYCHOTHERAPY	$103.00
90825	EVALUATION OF MEDICAL RECORDS	$104.00
90887	CASE CONFERENCE	$105.00
90899	LEGAL CONSULTATION- NS/C MISSED SESSION- OUTPATIENT PSYCHOTHERAPY	$106.00

CPT CODE	DESCRIPTION	AMNT
90801	PSYCHIATRIC DIAGNOSTIC INTERVIEW EXAMINATION	$107.00
90805	INDIVIDUAL PSYCHOTHERAPY, INSIGHT-ORIENTED 20/30 MIN W/MEDICAL EVALUATION AND MANAGEMENT SERVICES	$108.00
90807	INDIVIDUAL PSYCHOTHERAPY, INSIGHT-ORIENTED 45/50 MIN W/MEDICAL EVALUATION AND MANAGEMENT SERVICES	$109.00
90809	INDIVIDUAL PSYCHOTHERAPY, INSIGHT-ORIENTED 75/80 MINW/MEDICAL EVALUATION AND MANAGEMENT SERVICES	$110.00

CPT CODE	DESCRIPTION	AMNT
90809	INDIVIDUAL PSYCHOTHERAPY, INSIGHT-ORIENTED 75/80 MINW/MEDICAL EVALUATION AND MANAGEMENT SERVICES	$110.00
90862	PHARMACOLOGIC MANAGEMENT, INCLUDING PRESCRIPTION, USE AND REVIEW OF MEDICATION WITH NO MORE THAN MINIMAL PSYCHOTHERAPY	$111.00
M0064	MED CHECK ONLY INPATIENT HOSPITAL	$112.00
90816	INDIVIDUAL PSYCHOTHERAPY, INSIGHT-ORIENTED 20/30 MIN	$113.00
90818	INDIVIDUAL PSYCHOTHERAPY, INSIGHT-ORIENTED 45/50 MIN	$114.00

CPT CODE	DESCRIPTION	AMNT
90821	INDIVIDUAL PSYCHOTHERAPY, INSIGHT-ORIENTED 75/80 MIN	$115.00
99251-99255	INITIAL INPATIENT CONSULT SEE CPT FOR TIME INDICATIONS	$116.00

BILLING INSTRUCTIONS/COMMENTS:

_____

_____

_____

BILL PATIENT DIRECT ONLY

BILL INSURANCE ONLY-DO NOT BILL PATIENT

PRE-AUTH OBTAINED:

DATE _____ #SESSIONS_____ AUTH.
BY:_____ AUTH#: _____

Chapter 29

How Do I Get Doctors For My Business?

Well kiddies, marketing and sales is the last topic of discussion. This is an important and never ending task that <u>you will have to do</u> in order to become successful. Once you have implemented all the things you have learned in this book all you have to do is get your clients paid quickly and provide them with good customer service and your business will grow right before your eyes.

There are several avenues you can use to attract clientele such as:

Word of mouth

Networking (Chamber of Commerce, Billing Forums, Writing Articles Online, Answering Questions In Forums)

Monthly Mailings (Fliers, Brochures, Newsletters, Post Cards, Cooperative Mailings, etc.)

Daily Telemarketing

Cold calling

Email

Medical Journal/Publication Ads

Newspaper Ads

Gossip Magazine Ads

Create Website

Press Releases

The fact is when you are new you will not have the money to be able to partake in all these resources but you need to know that you have to be creative when you are trying to get clients from the very beginning.

As the market changes you will have to step-up your marketing campaign and separate yourself as a leader and expert in this industry if you want to expand your business.

There are also some roadblocks that you will encounter early on that will shake your perception of whether or not you will continue to pursue your dreams of opening a billing service such as:

Doctor's not wanting to take your calls

Office personnel blocking you from speaking to doctors

Getting no responses from your marketing and mailing campaigns

The overwhelming urge to stop telemarketing after the 30th "not interested" in a row

The fear of walking into a doctor's office to introduce yourself and service

Friends and family telling you that this business is not for you

Failing miserably in your first appointment with a doctor

Operating in the red (making no profits and still having to spend) for a long period of time and many other reasons.

Don't Panic! You have to take these things on the chin and work at overcoming the hardships you will experience (I told you this is not a get rich quick business). The good news is that if this is truly your passion you will find that through practice and reworking certain aspects of your natural skills you will become a master at building the perfect business (hey look at me, who would of thought I would one day start a business and then write a book in the process).

So how do you attract clientele on a small budget? I was told that the first thing I had to do was buy a mailing list of doctors from a database company, create a compelling sales letter or have someone (copywriter) create it for me, and mail it out to thousands of practitioners to introduce my services. Well, I did that.

The reality is by doing it I was just throwing stuff at a wall and hoping that it stuck (can you tell I'm still upset about following that advice)! Not only did that not work but I was also spending a lot of money I had not anticipated on spending which put my company further in the red. Now that I am little savvier I say you should do the following:

1. Before you get your business cards in your hands talk about the grand opening of your business to **everyone**. Start conversations with people wherever you are (online at the mall, supermarket, PTA meetings, church, chat rooms, etc.) with the hopes of speaking about what you do for a living (if that fails at least you made a new friend).

Attend block association or building association meetings to meet people in your neighborhood and mingle so they see who you are and talk about what you do. In short tell everyone and their mamma that you have started a medical billing business because people (if they like, trust, and see how knowledgeable and passionate you are) will refer business your way.

2. Once you have your business cards treat them like MasterCard (don't leave home without 'em). Hand them out like you're running for office and politic with everyone you come in contact with. Now, before you go overboard there has to be some method to your madness so before you give a card to the grocery bag boy make sure that he may be able to help you in your quest of getting clients.

Remember that sales is a numbers game that says the more people you introduce your product or service to, the more potential prospects you will get and all you have to do is get them to sign from there). Notice I have not said anything about doctors yet.

I just want you to get comfortable with speaking about your company and it's benefits to those you may or may not know so that you will gain confidence in yourself and your company. Plus it is a very inexpensive way to get the word out and hopefully you will bump into the mate or family member of a doctor that may be in need of your service.

You need to come up with a flyer that you will mail to physicians in you area. Unless you're a copywriter you will probably create a flyer that's cute but it will not entice a physician to consider doing business with you. Your advertising (all forms of it) has to mimic the way those major corporations entice you (an unidentified customer) to visit their department stores on a particular day, during a particular hour, to purchase a particular set of items or a better example would be those infomercials you see on TV.

Think of all the ads that have caught your attention (if you can't think of any just open a newspaper and scan it until you feel compelled to read a certain article).

All of these forms of advertising contain a few items that every piece of your marketing material should have in order to evoke a response from your targeted audience:

a) A compelling headline- This is the first line (headline) of your flier that a potential client will see. In our case, it must immed-iately grab the attention of the doctor and compel them to read further. It should highlight an issue that the doctor is going through (slow payments, reduced payments, compliance, ect).

b) The next line/paragraph should briefly expand or further explain that issue and then introduce the idea that the issue can be solved by implementing one of your company's techniques (it would be even more beneficial for you if you can back that up with a quote of a doctor or another authority that the doctor will trust). You can also use references from other doctors that you have worked with.

c) Then you go on to tell the reader of other benefits they would inherit by using your company and highlight them by the use of bullets.

d)You then wrap up with a call for action directing them to take the next step (another way of saying call me damn-it, but in a professional way).

e) Finally, give them your contact information (name, address, direct line, web page, and email) so they can act immediately while the thought is fresh in their minds.

You also have to realize that people do things quicker when they feel that they are going to get more than what they are going to put out. So be creative by using things like promotions, a report or subscription to a newsletter or journal about their specialty, money off your pricing, or anything you can think of that will add value too or make the practitioners life easier as ways of getting them to take notice of you.

CAUTION: don't give away the farm. Remember that you are in business to **make a sizable profit** and if you get in the practice of short changing yourself in order to get accounts it will become a habit (mentally) that you will not be able to break and will lead to you earning only a meager or non existent income.

Before I continue I just want to say that what I have covered here and on the next few pages only scratches the surface. However, since my mission is to give you the in-depth advice that you need here are the two resources I personally use to train my students in the topic of medical billing business marketing and sales:

Secrets To Signing Your First Doctor

budurl.com/getmedbillingclients

12 Medical Billing Marketing Strategies

budurl.com/marketingabillingbiz

Chapter 30

Do You Have An Example Of A Marketing Flyer?

Sure I do (don't I always supply you with an example). A doctor told me he had attended a physician's seminar and a major concern that was raised had to do with their practice's earning so much less than usual even though their patronage had increased.

He went on to say that the speaker asked the physicians how many of them were aware of the amount of money that hasn't been accounted for (held up because of unprocessed claims, denied claims, appealed claims, overdue accounts, and outstanding patient payments).

To the speakers surprise only seven physicians had a grasp of what was going on within their practice with regard to their accounts receivables. The speaker then told the remaining physician's that if they were to add up all the outstanding funds from the reasons mentioned above that they would come within 5-10% of what the practice should have made. As for the seven doctors that had an good idea of their A/R statements he suggested they hold a meeting with their billing supervisors and give them a week to compile the following information:

A report on all unprocessed and denied claims,

A report on all appeals in process along with the start dates the appeals were submitted,

A report of all of the denied claims within the year and any correspondence with the insurance company,

A report on the total of all outstanding patient accounts by 30-60-90 days (aging report) and

A report of the sum and total that is associated with the above discrepancies.

Then once that is complete hold a meeting with the billing supervisor and the billers and ask what problems they are experiencing that is holding up the total amount. Once the reasons are established a plan has to be put in place to capture the unclaimed funds in order to bring the practice up to date fiscally.

Then the supervisor has to draft and implement rules that the billing staff must follow to avoid falling behind again. Ok, let me stop there. What does this have to do with the sample flier?

Well in this case we see that several doctors are experiencing the same problems and that one way to get them current would be to outsource the current insurance claim volume so the billing staff can focus on past issues of recovering income.

This could serve as the basis of your flyer. Another way to look at it is if the physician were to outsource the unprocessed older claims (backlogged claims), the follow-up on the denied claims, and the follow-up of the overdue appeals then it would allow his staff to focus on incoming claims and the outstanding patient payments that need to be collected. This could also be the basis of a flyer. Either way you are solving the problem that all the physicians are experiencing; a reduction in their bottom line due to internal problems.

So, you could put together a flier that would look like the one on the following page.

Is Your Practice Seeing More Patients But Depositing Less Revenue?

Only 30% of physicians around the nation realize that the decrease in revenues that they are experiencing is an internal issue. Most practices are inundated with backlogged claims, uncontested denied claims, unresolved appealed claims, and uncollected patient payments that are eating away at the practices accounts receivables.

Is this happening in your practice? You can recover the unclaimed revenue you are legally entitled to without any further delay, stress on you and your staff, and without spending thousands to do it.

By implementing (name of your company) into your practices routine you will immediately:

Gain Peace of Mind- Only (whatever credentials you may have- CPC, CCS, RHIT, RHIA) will handle, submit, follow-up, appeal, and conduct the A/R and collection functions for your practice. Each biller/coder has a combination of at least 4 years of solo, group, and hospital experience.

Increase Productivity- (The name of your company) is at your disposal from 7AM-8PM weekdays and 7AM-6PM on Saturday. (The name of your company) will work twice as hard to get you reimbursed so that we too will become successful.

Increase Monthly Revenue Stream & Decrease Rejections- (The name of your company) mimics the payors standards to insure prompt payment to your location within 14-21 days. We also vigorously appeal every denied claim and aggressively but tactfully pursue all patients that have outstanding balances.

(The name of your company) will decrease your rejection rate to 2% by error checking each claim twice to ensure that all your claims are clean before submittal.

Take the First Step Toward Implementing a Sound Compliance Program

(The name of your company) follows a strict compliance program and have connections with (whatever organizations that you get information from -CMS, OIG, GAO, AAPC, etc.) for weekly updates to help keep you abreast of the ever-changing rules, mandates and regulations.

Get the First 30 Days Processing for FREE!!!

Our goal is to **Increase Your Practices Profitability By 20%** during the course of the first year and this is our first step in doing so. Pick up the phone and contact us immediately and together will improve your cash flow instantly!

(The Name of Your Company)

Phone: (***) ***-**** ♦ Fax: (***) ***-****

Full Address

Web Site: Email:

Depending on the type of publishing program (Adobe PageMaker, Publisher 2002, Quark, and Corel Ventura) that you use you will have the ability to create different types of fliers and marketing materials such as:

Single pages (flyers)

Newsletters

Pamphlets

Tri-Fold and

Postcards

Remember that you can also add images to liven up your materials to give it more impact. Do whatever you can to implant your name and services into the mind of your prospective client but do it profess-ionally (don't go overboard with the cuteness).

Once you make some funds from your clients you can invest in other forms of printed advertising like putting your name and logo on:

Tee shirts (jerseys, jackets, hats, etc.)

Pens

Sticky pads

Mouse pads

Coffee cups

Magnets and

Stickers

Repetition is the key when it comes to advertising.

Make quite a few mailers because you don't want to bore your prospective clients. **Do a mailing every month without fail** as to keep your name and services in the minds of every doctor and office manager that you contact.

Keep track of which mailer you sent out so that you don't send the same mailer twice in a row.

Most importantly follow up on your mailings with a phone call. The mailer is just an opening for you to <u>actually speak</u> to either the office manager or the physician. So instead of you making a cold call you will be able to say that you have been in contact with the practice before and you are following up on the correspondence that you sent.

Speaking of tracking. You should track the effectiveness of your mailings. By this I mean use either colored paper, a tracking number, or promotion code to distinguish your flyers so when a doctor calls you can ask which piece of material peeked his interest.

For example:

When a doctor calls, you should ask them how they heard of your company. If the response is I received a brochure then ask them the code you placed in the bottom right corner (or wherever you put it) of the mailing and that should coincide with one of your mailers.

Then you should record your findings so you know exactly which mailer is getting the most responses so that you can refer to it and use that as the basis for all future mailers (<u>because it is proven to evoke a response</u>).

The trick is to find out what works and use the premise over and over again in your work.

At the same time have fun and be very creative because not following the norm is why you decided to start your own business. The sky is the limit (oh that's right, as medical billers/entrepreneurs we don't have any limitations).

Chapter 31

I Made The Fliers. Now What?

The obvious answer is to mail them to physicians, right? Of course it is, but remember somewhere in the beginning I told you to become in tune with your computer, its software/programs and their functions? This is one reason why.

Before you embark on your quest of mailing out your brochures and advertising you first have to compile the addresses, phone numbers, the contact names and titles of the physicians and office personnel you are soliciting.

This way you will be able to re-contact them on a monthly basis without having to redo the research and you will be able to add new information as you get it.

You will also be able to build a personal report with the practice, which will form a good work ethic and trust (on your behalf) between you, the practice, and the staff.

If your computer does not have a database program or contact management program such as Excel, ACT, Goldmine, Maximizer, Microsoft Outlook, Microsoft Access, or Lotus Notes it would be best to invest in acquiring it (and this can be expensive).

I understand that it is going to add to the amount that you have already spent but this will allow you to work smarter - not harder.

If you are entirely strapped for cash you can go to sites such as:

www.cnet.com

Click on the download link located at the very top of the left hand portion of the page and when the page loads input what kind of software you are in need of such as; "contact management", Marketing Manager, or VicMan's Database.
(some of the downloadable software is free and others are 30 day trials with an upgrade to ownership for a specific charge.)

www.zdnet.com

Click on the download link located at the top of the right hand portion of the page and when the page loads input what kind of software you are in need of such as; "contact management", Reach-Out 2.5, or Contact Manager Deluxe 1.0. Again most of the downloadable software is free, others are demos only, and some are 30 day trials with an upgrade to ownership for a specific charge.

Research the listings at both sites, download different software titles, and learn how to use them. Once you feel comfortable with the func-tions of a database you will know exactly which software would be best for your business and stick with that.

Chapter 32

Where Do I Find The Contact Information For A Physician?

1. Start by opening up your contact management program, then open your local phone book to the physician's/doctor's section and input all the contact information. For the listings that give only partial information just input what you can and call the doctors office later for the rest.

2. If you have belonged to an insurance program from work and still have the book with the participating physicians use that to acquire their contact information.

3. If you have a connection to the Internet look up doctors, physicians and then do a search by specialty (chiropractors, surgeons, dermatologists, podiatrists, etc.) for the info. Take all the email addresses you find and start an email database and solicit doctors in the middle of the month during your regular mailing cycle (include the words "If you no longer want to receive updates from us please hit reply and place "remove" in the subject area".

Place it visibly at the bottom so it is not overlooked and you are accused of spamming which can lead to you losing your ISP). The emails should emulate your mailers in content but be very brief.

4. Use the information that you already have like your family physician or any physician that you have seen in the past.

5. Ask your friends and family for the contact information to any doctor they may know or have visited in the past.

6. Ask your accountant if they have dealt with any practices/physicians that have complained about their financial situation and ask them to refer you. You might have come up with an incentive for them to do it or you could propose including their marketing material in your mailings for added exposure for their company (cooperative marketing).

7. Go to or join your local Chamber of Commerce and go to their meetings and network with others in your neighborhood. This is a valuable resource because you will be face to face with business owners of all types that have the potential to refer or help you expand your business.

8. Join in on medical billing and network or answer questions that they may have concerning healthcare reimbursement. When you answer a question sign it and include a link to your web page and email address so if a physician is impressed with your knowledge they can contact you.

Lastly, you could purchase a list of doctors from a reputable marketing company (notice I put this last because you have to spend money and it's hard to distinguish who is reputable in that industry). You should use as many forms of attracting physicians as you can and contact them once a month.

Chapter 33

Is That All I Have To Do To Get Doctors?

Not exactly (my associates might think otherwise). If you try to just solicit doctors by mail there is something you should know. The national direct mail response rate is about a 1-3% so if you want to heighten your odds of attracting clients quicker you will have to cold-call and telemarket.

I know many of you are not going to like doing this because of fear, the thought of making a fool of yourself and coming face-to-face with rejection. The only thing that I can say is you will encounter all of the above but if you continue cold-calling and telemarketing you will overcome the initial fear, develop a thick skin, and develop a talk track worthy of a proud business owner. When you get the willies just shake them off by telling yourself that the call could turn into a lead that will eventually translate into big bucks.

You will have to take a deep breath, calm down, visualize how and what you are going to say, and pretend that you already know those people but haven't seen them in a while. This will allow you to walk in with a smile on your face and you will sound more confident than you actually are.

Once you're in you don't have to spend an eternity trying to question the already busy personnel, or overwhelm them with your services and how you can help them, and putting the added pressure on yourself to keep the conversation lively.

Whether this is your first time into an office or speaking on the phone you only need to do the following:

1. Smile (it makes your voice more friendly and less threatening)

2. Walk in (maintain eye contact with the person behind the desk)

3. Introduce yourself and your company while handing them your business card

4. Ask the receptionist their name and permission to speak with the office manager

5. Introduce yourself to the office manager and get their name

Tell the office manager:

a) You are a new medical billing company in the area

b) You are visiting as many physicians as you can to let them know that you exist

c) That you specialize in part time and full time backlogged and present electronic claims processing, coding, billing, follow-up, collections and A/R functions and that you could be of service to the practice when their billing personnel is on vacation, sick, or when the position is open.

d) Ask them if they have a billing staff or if they outsource their billing

e) Give them your brochure, a business card and ask that they keep you in mind if a situation should arise

f) Then thank them for their time, shake their hand, and while walking away stop and ask one last question (like Colombo does just before he walks out after questioning someone) which is:

Are you aware of a practice in the area that might be in need of your services right now?

g) Thank them again and you're outta' there.

I told you before that sales is a numbers game so you should plan to do a certain amount of telemarketing calls a day and cold calls per week and make that a standard routine. <u>For example:</u>

30 cold calls every Monday-Wednesday- and Friday will equal 90 cold calls a week, 360 per month, and 4320 per year. 70 phone calls per day Monday-Friday will equal 350 calls a week, 1400 per month, and 16,800 per year.

In both cases statistics show that you should get at least 1 interested client per every 60 calls. Therefore by doing the above will net you about 7 interested clients per week, 28 per month and 336 per year. Doesn't that sound great?

Before you get carried away you have to realize that out of the 336 interested clients statistic show that less than half of them will turn into appointments. Out of those appointments about less than half will actually get to the point of closing depending on your individual close rate (the amount of potential clients that you can convince to sign a contract). The good thing is even if you only close12 practitioners out of the remaining 84 potential clients in that year you could be well on your way to a sizable profit.

You will hear **many** rejections or we're not interested but **you have to continue with the mission at hand** because during your calls you will bump into a practice that will praise you for stopping by or calling (this is one of the best feelings in the world besides getting a signature on a contract so work toward it).

Chapter 34

Do you Have Any Other Advice?

Well, I have gone over mailers, telemarketing, and cold-calling because these are going to be your front line approaches at getting clients. There a few other outlets that I believe should also be incorporated into your efforts as time goes on and as you begin to earn a profit pay for them (unless you're rich already and just doing this as a hobby).

1. You need to place an advertisement in your local telephone book and the surrounding the counties.

2. Increase you mailings to include physicians in other counties and then out of state.

3. Become corporate members of different organizations and attend meetings regularly (especially in other states. This will give you a break from the house, the family, and give you an opportunity to meet new people and see new places).

4. Write articles about things that physicians are experiencing, introduce solutions to healthcare management problems and submit them to medical publications and organizations.

5. Create a web page worthy of your success and corporate identity.

6. Continue your education and become certified in every aspect of the healthcare management field as possible.

Personal Note

In my quest to keep this book educational, entertaining and inexpensive I was not able to drill down into certain topics as much as I would have liked to. To rectify this issue I created the following webpage to cover:

Medical Billing Business In A Box

Secrets To Signing Up Your First Doctor

How To Market Your Medical Billing Business

Chiropractic Billing Made Easy

Mental Health Billing Big Pack

How To Correctly Complete A CMS 1500 Form

How To Complete A UB04 Form

Start A Work At Home Medical Transcription Career

Go Online Right Now & Bookmark The Following Webpage In Your Browser Because You Will Need To Refer To It In The Future:

medicalbillingbooks.tripod.com/medicalbillingresources.html

Now that I have covered all of the incidentals **are you ready to get started? Then let's get going!**

Appendix A

Checklist for Starting a Medical Billing Business

Assess your strengths and weaknesses

Establish business and personal goals

Assess your financial resources

Identify the financial risks

Determine the start-up costs

Decide on your business location

Do market research

Identify your customers

Identify your competitors

Develop a marketing plan

Select a lawyer

Choose a form of organization (proprietorship, partnership, or corporation, for example)

Create your business (register your name, incorporate the business, etc.)

Select an accountant

Prepare a business plan

Select a banker

Set up a business checking account

Apply for business loans (if applicable)

Establish a line of credit

Select an insurance agent

Obtain business insurance

Get business cards

Review local business codes

Line up suppliers (if applicable)

Get furniture and equipment

Obtain a business license or permit (if applicable)

Get a federal employer identification number (if applicable)

Get a state employer I.D. number (if applicable)

Send for federal and state tax forms

Join a professional organization

Set a starting date

Research software vendors/companies

Research educational programs

Obtain software demo/evaluation copies

Research Clearinghouses

Setup phone/fax/modem lines (separate is preferred)

Order forms, coding books, other office necessities

Create letterhead, brochures and stationery

Prepare or obtain mailing lists

Input or import leads to contact management Software

Prepare and mail your marketing materials

Track and follow-up on all mailings

Appendix B

Must Read Medical Billing Resources (In-Depth Topics)

As I have said again and again, my mission was to be brief in this ebook while covering all the topics you need to know right now to get you started correctly. However, the following ebooks go in-depth into the topics that I was not able to drill down into as much as I would have liked:

Medical Billing Home Business In A Box

5 medical billing ebooks, 3 billing manuals, 3 special reports, 2 insiders secrets reports, a free one-on-one phone consultation with a medical billing business expert and a carrying case to keep everything organized.

budurl.com/medicalbillingboxset

Secrets To Signing Up Your First Doctor

Everything you need to know before you step foot into the first doctors office.

budurl.com/getmedbillingclients

How To Market Your Medical Billing Business

12 proven marketing strategies to sell and market your business (it includes phone scripts, letters, and other resources).

budurl.com/marketingabillingbiz

The Basics Of Medical Billing

This ebook was really meant for correctly training the office staff of a doctors office.

However, I recommend it to my readers because If you know all the shortcomings that the back office staff can experience then it would be easy for you to spot the problems and use that knowledge to your advantage to secure their business.

budurl.com/medicalbillingbasics

Chiropractic Billing Made Easy

Everything You Need To Know about Chiropractic billing, submitting of claims and getting properly reimbursed for your services.

budurl.com/chiropracticbilling

Mental Health Billing Big Pack

Everything you need to know about doing mental health billing, with 20 Completcd Claims along with answer key and includes a very special bonus.

budurl.com/mentalhealthbilling

Big Pack Of Sample Completed CMS 1500 Forms

Package of 20 Correctly Completed Mental Health CMS 1500 Forms, with answer Keys explaining every Claim, and a list of the most common denials.

budurl.com/CompletedCMS1500Samp

Expanding Your Medical Billing Business

Everything you need to know about growing and expanding your medical billing business.

budurl.com/expandyourbillingbiz

How To Correctly Complete A CMS 1500 Form

Prevent silly denials by learning exactly how to fill the form out correctly.

budurl.com/howtocompletecms1500

How To Complete A UB04 Form

Prevent silly denials by learning exactly how to fill the form out correctly.

budurl.com/howtocompleteaub04

Start A Work At Home Medical Transcription Career

Starting a work at home medical transcription business is easier than starting a home based medical billing business and unlike medical billing you can contract with local and regional companies that will hire you to transcribe their overflow of workload.

budurl.com/mtathomeebook

Appendix C

Medical Billing Forums

I suggest that you pay for one of the yearly memberships to the organizations denoted with a *. You will receive up-to-date information about the healthcare industry, network with other successful billers, get unlimited marketing resources, etc.

*Cyndee Weston- President of the **American Medical Billing Association***

www.webcom.com/medical/AMBA.htm

* Linda Walker – Presidents of **Practice Managers Resource & Networking Community***

www.billerswebsite.com

*Liz Jones-**Medical Association of Billers***

www.physicianswebsites.com & www.e-medbill.com

National Medical Billers Alliance

www.nebazone.com

ScamWatch

View all the posts/topics especially under the title "Is It Hype? or Is It Legit?").

medicalbillingscamwatch.yuku.com

Appendix D

Medial Billing Instruction Directory

My #1 Pick For Medical Billing Certification Training
9 Module Home Study Course-Certificate Program-it's the best

budurl.com/medicalbillingcourse

Medical Association Of Billers
8 Module Home Study Course and Certification Exam
www.e-medbill.com/

American Medical Billing Association
Certified Medical Reimbursement Specialist Exam
www.webcom.com/medical/AMBA.htm

Practice Managers Resource & Networking Community
HIPAA & Compliance Courses = www.billerswebsite.com/

American Academy of Professional Coders

CPC, CPC-H = www.aapc.com/

American Health Information Management Association

(2 year College Degree-RHIT) (4 Year College Degree-RHIA)
(12 Module Home Study Course-then take test for the CCS,
CCS-P) = www.ahima.org/

Appendix E

Software Companies

Software & Website	Phone Number
Lytec www.lytec.com	(800) 735-1991
Medisoft www.medisoft.com	(800) 333-4747
PMX3 www.synergymis.com	(800) 652-3500
AS/PC www.dbconsultants.com	(610) 847-5065
HP Plus Pro www.healthpac.net	(800) 831-9419

Software & Website	Phone Number
AltaPoint www.altapoint.com	(888) 258-2552
Kareo **(Web Based)** www.kareo.com	(888) 775-2736
Visionary www.visionarymed.com	(888) 895-2466
DAQ Billing www.antekhealthware.com	(800) 359-0911 (Ext.# 5)

Appendix F

Medical Billing Opportunities

Company & Website	Phone Number
Claims Transit www.ambanet.net/info.htm	(580) 622-5809
Synergy MIS www.synergymis.com/	(800) 652-3500
ClaimTek www.claimtek.com	(800) 224-7450
Pacific Medical www.pacificmedical.com	(800) 815-6334
Medical Billing Business Resources www.medicalbillingbusiness resources.com/	(865) 286-9124 (Ext.# 13)

Appendix G

Clearinghouse Directory

Company & Website	Phone Number
Claimsnet.com www.claimsnet.com	(800) 356-1511
DataClaim www.dataclaim.com	(888) 328-2252
ET&T Clearinghouse www.ettch.com	(480) 325-0901
Medi.com www.medi.com	(888) 334-6278
MedAvant www.medavanthealth.com	(800) 882-0802

Appendix H

Business Name / Business Plan/ Business Law Resources

U.S. Patent and Trademark Office = www.uspto.gov/

Knowx = www.knowx.com

Dunn & Bradstreet = sbs.dnb.com/

If you are going to put your business online it would be best to check if your business name can be acquired as a domain name at:

Network Solutions = www.networksolutions.com/cgi-bin/whois/whois

To establish a corporation you use either Incorporation.com or use a CPA or an attorney to do it:

InCorporation.com = www.corporate.com/cgi-bin/a.pl?compcorp&9195

To get a sample medical billing company business plan go to:
www.bplans.com/medical_billing_business_plan/executive_summary_fc.cfm

Appendix I

Government Agencies You Need To Know To Get Up To Date Information

Compliance

oig.hhs.gov/fraud/docs/complianceguidance/thirdparty.pdf

www.hipaadvisory.com/

www.hipaa.org/

www.hipaacomply.com/

OIG = oig.hhs.gov/

Health Care Financing Administration (HCFA/CMS)

cms.hhs.gov/

Medicare Part A: CT, DE, MA & NY or Part B: NJ or Part B: NY = www.empiremedicare.com/

Acknowledgements

I would like to give thanks to the following people and organizations that gave me the courage and assistance I needed in the last 13 years to accurately help others start, open and operate their own home based medical billing and transcription business:

Sandra L. Swies, HRS.- President of **SES Physicians Management & Medical Billing Help Center**

Tammy Harlan- President of **MedicalBillingCourse.com & MedicalBillingBusinessResources.com**

Linda Walker- President of **Practice Managers Resource & Networking Community**

Cyndee Weston- President of the **American Medical Billing Association**

All those at the **Small Business Administration**

All those at the **Service Corps Of Retired Executives**

Thank You!!!

Thank You For Purchasing The Medical Billing Home Business Bible!

I hope it has given you the answers you were looking for and answered some questions that you never thought of or even knew you should ask.

Please Feel Free To Contact Me At One The Following:

Paul Hackett
The Medical Billing & Transcription Mastermind

90-39 179th Place

Suite# 2B

Jamaica Estates, NY 11432

stelopm@nyc.rr.com

medicalbillingbooks.tripod.com

CPSIA information can be obtained at www.ICGtesting.com
Printed in the USA
LVOW050537090712

289268LV00001B/57/P